MW01052243

Understanding How We Learn

Educational practice does not, for the most part, rely on research findings. Instead, there's a preference for relying on our intuitions about what's best for learning. But relying on intuition may be a bad idea for teachers and learners alike.

This accessible guide shows how to integrate effective, research-backed strategies for learning into classroom practice. The book explores exactly what constitutes good evidence for effective learning and teaching strategies, how to make evidence-based judgments instead of relying on intuition, and how to apply findings from cognitive psychology directly to the classroom.

Including real-life examples and case studies, FAQs, and a wealth of engaging illustrations to explain complex concepts and emphasize key points, the book is divided into four parts:

- Evidence-based education and the science of learning
- Basics of human cognitive processes
- Strategies for effective learning
- Tips for students, teachers, and parents.

Written by "The Learning Scientists" Drs. Yana Weinstein and Megan Sumeracki and fully illustrated by Oliver Caviglioli, *Understanding How We Learn* is a rejuvenating and fresh examination of cognitive psychology's application to education. This is an essential read for all teachers and educational practitioners, designed to convey the concepts of research to the reality of a teacher's classroom.

Yana Weinstein is Assistant Professor of Psychology at University of Massachusetts Lowell, USA. Yana is co-founder of The Learning Scientists, http://www.learningscientists.org/, a project whose goal is to make scientific research on learning more accessible to students, teachers, and other educators. Yana tweets as @doctorwhy.

Megan Sumeracki (formerly Smith) is Assistant Professor of Psychology at Rhode Island College, USA. Megan is co-founder of The Learning Scientists, where she aims to increase the use of effective study and teaching strategies that are backed by research. Megan tweets as @DrSumeracki.

Oliver Caviglioli was a principal of a special school for a decade, before co-creating the HOW2s– visual guides to evidence-based teaching techniques. More recently, Oliver has used a variety of visual formats in different contexts: hand-drawn sketchnotes, digital diagrams, infographics, live hand-drawn conference notes and posters. Oliver is busy on Twitter as @olivercavigliol.

Understanding How We Learn

A Visual Guide

Yana Weinstein and Megan Sumeracki

with Oliver Caviglioli

Routledge
Taylor & Francis Group

LONDON AND NEW YORK

First published 2019
by Routledge
2 Park Square, Milton Park, Abingdon, Oxon OX14 4RN

and by Routledge
711 Third Avenue, New York, NY 10017

Routledge is an imprint of the Taylor & Francis Group, an informa business

British Library Cataloguing-in-Publication Data
A catalogue record for this book is available from the British Library

Library of Congress Cataloging-in-Publication Data
Names: Weinstein, Yana, author. | Sumeracki, Megan, author. | Caviglioli, Oliver, author.
Title: Understanding how we learn : a visual guide / Yana Weinstein,
    Megan Sumeracki, and Oliver Caviglioli.
Description: Abingdon, Oxon ; New York, NY : Routledge, 2019. |
    Includes bibliographical references.
Identifiers: LCCN 2018013568 (print) | LCCN 2018028126 (ebook) |
    ISBN 9780203710463 (ebook) | ISBN 9781138561694 (hbk) |
    ISBN 9781138561724 (pbk) | ISBN 9780203710463 (ebk)
Subjects: LCSH: Learning, Psychology of. | Cognitive learning. | Effective teaching.
Classification: LCC LB1060 (ebook) | LCC LB1060 .W44 2019 (print) |
    DDC 370.15/23—dc23
LC record available at https://lccn.loc.gov/2018013568

ISBN: 978-1-138-56169-4 (hbk)
ISBN: 978-1-138-56172-4 (pbk)
ISBN: 978-0-203-71046-3 (ebk)

Typeset in Plantin and Helvetica Neue
by Apex CoVantage, LLC

Contents

PART 1

EVIDENCE-BASED EDUCATION AND THE SCIENCE OF LEARNING

PART 2

BASICS OF HUMAN COGNITIVE PROCESSES

PART 3

STRATEGIES FOR EFFECTIVE LEARNING

ACKNOWLEDGMENTS

We would like to thank the Association for Psychological Science, IDEA Education, the Overdeck Family Foundation, and the Wellcome Trust for supporting the Learning Scientists project and helping us to create resources for teachers and students to promote learning. We would also like to thank University of Massachusetts Lowell and Rhode Island College for their support.

We also wish to thank the other researchers on our Learning Scientists team, Cindy Nebel and Carolina Kuepper-Tetzel, who have been wonderful collaborators and friends as well as the numerous teachers, researchers, and other educators who have contributed to our understanding of how we learn, many of whom appear throughout the book.

Yana would like to thank her PhD and postdoc mentors David Shanks, Roddy Roediger, and Kathleen McDermott, who have supported her work for the past decade. Megan would also like to thank her graduate advisors, Roddy Roediger and Jeff Karpicke.

We would like to thank those students in our research labs at University of Massachusetts Lowell and Rhode Island College who continue to contribute to active research on student learning. Students working with Yana Weinstein on science of learning projects are PhD students Meltem Karaca and Marcus Lithander, who feature in Chapter 4 with undergraduate research assistant Shannon Rowley, as well as undergraduate student Annmarie Khairalla who worked on the book's glossary. Students working with Megan Sumeracki are Master's student Carissa DiPietro and undergraduates Ashley Bazin, Giselle Colon, Elizabeth Greenleaf, and Audrianna Vito. We also wish to thank countless students who have helped directly with the Learning Scientists project, including Rachel Adragna, Emily Castonguay, Elizabeth Greenleaf, Syeda Nizami, and Amalie Ducasse.

Yana would like to thank her husband, Fabian Weinstein-Jones, for enthusiastically embracing all of her ideas and projects, and her four children Aurelia, Katelyn, Ethan, and Fabian for listening to her talk incessantly about learning strategies.

Megan would like to thank her husband, Samuel Sumeracki, for being so loving and supportive. He has contributed to the Learning Scientists project in invaluable ways. She also thanks her mom, Sandy Stuck, who always made sure her life was full of learning.

Finally, we would like to thank Alice Gray, Annamarie Kino, and Clare Ashworth, our editors, and other helpful staff at Routledge for guidance and support during the writing and editing of this book.

Oliver would like to thank his wife, Lyn – now three years retired from teaching – who still has to put up with his incessant babblings about such and such a teaching strategy. Her support has often veered towards suffering.

AUTHOR PROFILE

Dr. Megan Sumeracki   Dr. Yana Weinstein

WHO ARE YOU?

We are two cognitive psychologists who do applied research in education.

Yana first got hooked on "false memory."

Yana:

False memory is something I learned about in my first undergraduate research methods class: the idea that we sometimes remember things that did not occur, or differently to how they really occurred. I got stuck on the idea that surely there is an objectively "true" memory somewhere in our minds that we distinguish from this "false" memory. My dream was that you could take a person who claimed to have a particular memory, do some clever science on them, and come back with a "TRUE!" or "FALSE!" indicator for that particular memory. What can I say – I was young and naïve. I tried to research this in my PhD, but realized too late that it was, in fact, more or less impossible to distinguish

between true and false memories with a cognitive task. I then went on to join Henry (Roddy) Roediger's lab, where I learned all about how to apply memory research to education. Now my passion has shifted over to figuring out the best way for students to learn, based on advances in cognitive psychology and our understanding of how the mind processes and remembers information.

Megan got into cognitive research as an undergraduate student because she was interested in education.

Megan:

By the beginning of my junior year in college I was getting ready to apply for the research-focused honors program at Purdue University, and had started subbing K-12 on days when I didn't have classes – I went to great lengths to block them off so that I would have two full days off at a time. I loved being in the classroom and working with students, and I loved issues related to education. I applied to conduct my honors thesis in Jeff Karpicke's Learning Lab (http://learninglab.psych.purdue.edu/people/karpicke/), where I started conducting my own applied research on learning. I fell in love with the research, and continued to pursue training in cognitive psychology and applications to education. I had found my passion, and wanted to have a role in changing education.

WHAT KIND OF RESEARCH DO YOU DO?

Yana:

My research interests lie in improving the accuracy of memory performance and the judgments students make about their cognitive functions. I try to pose questions that have direct applied relevance, such as: How can we help students choose optimal study strategies? Why are test scores sometimes so surprising to students? And how does retrieval practice help students learn?

Megan:

My area of expertise is in human learning and memory, and applying the science of learning in educational contexts. My research program focuses on retrieval-based learning strategies, and the way activities promoting retrieval can improve meaningful learning in the classroom. I address empirical questions such as: What retrieval practice formats promote student learning? What retrieval practice activities work well for different types of learners? And, why does retrieval increase learning?

WHY ARE YOU WRITING THIS BOOK?

We are writing this book to continue the conversation about evidence-based learning strategies that we started on our website and blog, learningscientists.org, and our Twitter account, @AceThatTest. When we started the Learning Scientists, it was because we wanted to make the cognitive psychology research on learning more accessible, to increase its ability to have real positive impacts for students around the world. Essentially, we have aimed to break out of the typical walls of academic research and talk about research and education with many relevant parties, and not just our fellow researchers.

HOW DID YOU START THE LEARNING SCIENTISTS PROJECT?

Yana:

One night in January 2016, I was feeling guilty about not doing enough to disseminate my research on learning to students — so I decided to see what I could do on Twitter. I searched "test tomorrow" and realized that many students tweet about how unprepared they feel for their upcoming exams or about how they can't concentrate enough to study. I began tweeting advice at these students.

Megan:

At the same time, I had started a new professional Twitter account and was trying to create an assignment for my students in cognitive psychology where they would find articles and tweet them. The assignment was a slight disaster, but in the process, Yana and I connected again (we had crossed over at Washington University in St. Louis, but had not worked together directly), and I saw what she was doing and started joining in. And then I realized if my account was flooded with all of this stuff, my students were going to get confused, so I suggested that maybe we should start our own Twitter handle just for this. That's when the Learning Scientists Twitter account (@AceThatTest) was born. At the time of writing, we now have over 10,000 followers, and the project has grown to so much more than just a Twitter account. We have a thriving blog, multiple funded research and science communication projects, a podcast, and now this book.

WHAT DRIVES YOU?

We're passionate about education and giving people tools to study and teach more effectively.

WHAT MIGHT YOU HOPE THE READER WILL DO WITH THE KNOWLEDGE?

Apply it to their own lives – after all, everyone is trying to learn something!

ILLUSTRATOR PROFILE

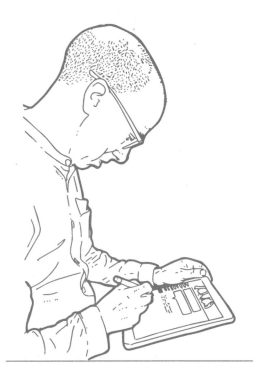

Oliver Caviglioli

WHO ARE YOU?

I'm a former special school principal who, from childhood, has been interested in visual communication. My architect father introduced me to diagrams, typography, and the fine arts in general. So when I became a special school teacher, this focus on visual depiction served me well, and by working with educational psychologists for a number of decades, I found an increasingly useful range of applications for my growing set of skills.

HOW DO YOU USE YOUR VISUALS TO AID LEARNING?

In addition to illustrating books, I also create posters and slide presentations, as well as designing documents. Then there's something called sketchnotes. These are live notes made of presentations at conferences. Or, alternatively – and rather less stressful – they can be hand-drawn summaries of book chapters, for example. Napkin sketches are similarly hand-drawn, but focus on depicting either the structure of concepts or stages of processes. They are immensely helpful in analyzing and depicting the steps involved in teaching techniques.

HAVE YOU WORKED WITH THE LEARNING SCIENTISTS BEFORE?

Yes, last year we collaborated in the creation of a set of posters of the top six learning strategies as identified by cognitive psychology. The posters have now been translated into a dozen languages and can be found on classroom walls around the globe.

WHAT DO YOU GET OUT OF WORKING WITH THE LEARNING SCIENTISTS?

I end up getting the most marvelous education! As we discuss how best to visually explain some pieces of research, for example, I receive explanations that are personalised to my level of understanding. Being able to ask questions until you think you have established a good understanding is a treat, as well as being essential for creating the illustrations. And, of course, the illustrations become feedback to Yana and Megan on the effectiveness of their explanations. A perfect loop in which to learn!

Part 1

EVIDENCE-BASED EDUCATION
AND THE SCIENCE OF LEARNING

COMMUNICATION BREAKDOWN BETWEEN SCIENCE AND PRACTICE IN EDUCATION

Western medicine: a drug is proposed, tested by science, found to be better than a placebo and put on the market.

We advocate that teaching and learning strategies be put to the test, as in the medical field.

Alarmingly, our feelings about how we learn can often be more compelling than reality.

In many cases, going with our intuition about how we learn can be detrimental.

Very few teacher education courses cover principles of cognitive psychology related to learning.

Teacher-training textbooks and courses sometimes propagate misunderstandings about learning.

The discrepancy between research and practice is a lot more than just a communication breakdown.

There are a number of reasons why teachers may not be inclined to engage in evidence-based practice.

We want to open up the lines of communication between researchers, teachers, and students.

COMMUNICATION BREAKDOWN BETWEEN SCIENCE AND PRACTICE IN EDUCATION

Unfortunately, educational practice does not, for the most part, rely on research findings. Instead, we tend to rely on our intuitions about how to teach and learn – with detrimental consequences.

In 1928 Alexander Fleming came back from vacation and accidentally discovered a colony of mold that led to the development of penicillin, which can be used against bacterial infections (Ligon, 2004). This process then took several decades and involved clinical trials where this new drug was compared to other drugs that, at the time, were thought to help fight bacterial infections (Abraham *et al.*, 1941). The model that we, as cognitive psychologists, are striving for in education is similar to the one exemplified by this anecdote, and used broadly in mainstream Western medicine: a drug is proposed, tested by science, found to be better than a placebo, and put on the market.

Western medicine: a drug is proposed, tested by science, found to be better than a placebo and put on the market.

Of course, any one drug does not work all the time, and so doctors will prescribe different drugs at different doses for different circumstances, conditions, and individuals.

However, Henry L. (Roddy) Roediger III reported in 2013 that, unfortunately, educational practice does not, for the most part, rely on research findings (of course, this is not always how medicine works, either; see Haynes, Devereaux, & Guyatt [2002] about how "evidence does not make decisions, people do").

Henry Roediger
Henry L. (Roddy) Roediger III, James S. McDonnell Distinguished University Professor of Psychology, Washington University in St. Louis

Instead, somewhat dubious sources of evidence such as untested theories – or, even worse, marketing ploys by financially interested parties – drive educational fads. This concern is not new. For example, back in 1977, Fred Kerlinger (an American educational psychologist born in 1910) gave a presidential address at the American Educational Research Association conference on this issue. He argued in particular that education should pay more attention to *basic* research – the type of research that aims to figure out how and why people learn and behave the way they do. In this book, we review important basic processes – perception, attention, and memory – but we also focus on *applied* research – research that takes what we know about basic processes and applies them to real-life educational questions and settings.

HOW DO WE KNOW WHETHER A TEACHING OR LEARNING STRATEGY IS EFFECTIVE?

We advocate that teaching and learning strategies be put to the test, as in the medical field.

If evidence supports the effectiveness of a strategy, then we should by all means adopt it, but continue to be flexible as the science evolves. After all, would you give your child a pill that had never been scientifically tested? Or worse, one that had been scientifically tested and was shown not to work? Would you bring your child to a doctor whose practice was based on opinion and intuition alone, rather than the most up-to-date science? We know we wouldn't. To use another example, think about the distinction between astrology and astronomy. Many of us know that one of those is science, and the other is … a fun pastime, at best.

Astronomy vs. astrology – one is science, the other is not.

However, when talking about something as broad as "learning," there are various different scientific fields that we can draw from. *In Chapter 2, we talk about different types of evidence about how we learn.* For the purposes of this book, we will be focusing on evidence from **cognitive psychology**, because that is our area of expertise. Cognitive psychology is usually defined as the study of the mind, including processes such as perception, attention, and memory (not to be confused with neuroscience, which focuses on how the brain functions). This field of research can help us understand learning by testing hypotheses about learning strategies that are developed based on what we already know about the mind.

A different type of evidence is our own intuition. Because often, our feelings about how we learn are more compelling than reality.

Alarmingly, our feelings about how we learn can often be more compelling than reality.

For example, if students read and re-read a textbook, they will become more and more confident that they will do well on a later test. If another group of students instead take practice tests, they will be less confident in their later performance – because these tests can feel hard. But in reality, those who took the practice tests will outperform those who re-read the textbook (see Chapter 9 for more about this technique).

In this case, and in many others, going with our intuition about how we learn can be detrimental.

Relying upon intuition, rather than science, can also lead us to latch on to false positives. There are certainly times when we see a positive result just because of luck or chance. But, this positive result does not mean that a particular method will work consistently over time. For an example, think about sports. If you're an American football fan, then you can probably remember a time when the quarterback made a long-haul pass down the field that was successfully caught and run into the end zone for a touchdown. But, we know these "hail Mary'" passes certainly don't work every time, and it would be a mistake to attempt the long-haul pass on every play. This would likely lead to an increase in losses for that team in the long run.

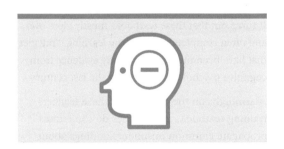

In many cases, going with our intuition about how we learn can be detrimental.

We will cover this scenario, and other learning scenarios where intuition can mislead us, in Chapter 3 and throughout the book.

Not only does our intuition often mislead our own selves, but often, we can end up misleading others, too. The concept of "learning styles" is one example of time, money, and energy spent on a practice that is not particularly good at increasing learning, according to the evidence

(Rohrer & Pashler, 2012). You may have heard of it: "learning styles" describe the idea that students learn best in different ways. The most popular of these "styles" are visual and verbal styles: the idea is that some people are visual learners, while others are verbal learners. Importantly, proponents of learning styles claim that in order to maximize student learning, we must "match" instruction to each individual's learning style (Flores, n.d.)

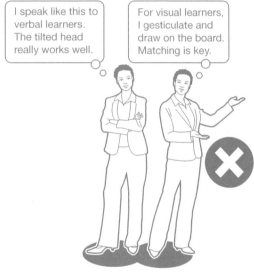

After a thorough review of the scientific literature, a group of leading researchers discovered that there was no evidence to support this view (Pashler, McDaniel, Rohrer, & Bjork, 2008). That is, there was not a single controlled experiment in the literature that demonstrated that matching instruction to learning styles overall helped students learn more. We talk more about this and other misunderstandings in Chapter 4. Above all, we do not want teachers and students finding themselves wasting time on strategies that are not particularly effective (see over).

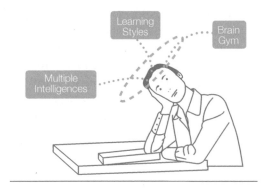

Trying to implement these strategies may not be the best use of our time.

Furthermore, according to a recent report (Pomerance, Greenberg, & Walsh, 2016), very few teacher education courses and textbooks in the US cover principles from cognitive psychology related to effective learning.

Very few teacher education courses cover principles of cognitive psychology related to learning.

WHAT DO TEACHERS AND STUDENTS LEARN ABOUT COGNITIVE PSYCHOLOGY?

We believe that researchers, teachers, and students should have an open dialogue about research related to learning. It is in everyone's best interest to talk to one another so that we can make the best use of recommendations from learning science in the classroom, and figure out what additional research would be most helpful for teachers and students. But how do those actually involved in teaching – and those involved in training teachers – feel about using cognitive psychology findings in their teaching practices?

Laski, Reeves, Ganley, and Mitchell (2013) asked trainers of elementary mathematics teachers across the US to what extent they found cognitive psychology to be important to teaching mathematics. While most found it important, very few of the respondents actually accessed the relevant primary sources (i.e., cognitive psychology journals). When asked how often teachers read cognitive journals to inform their teacher-training practice, the most frequent response was "Never." This response makes sense, as journal articles are dense, full of jargon, and often behind paywalls such that those outside of higher education do not typically have access.

This suggests that the six strategies that have received the most evidence from cognitive psychology – which we will cover in Chapters 8 through 10 – are not systematically making their way into the learning experience in the classroom.

It turns out that these textbooks mostly gloss over, and often completely ignore, the learning strategies that have been most supported by evidence from cognitive psychology throughout the last century.

Alarmingly, on the other hand, these teacher-training textbooks and courses do sometimes propagate common misunderstandings about learning, which we will talk about in Chapter 4.

Teacher-training textbooks and courses sometimes propagate misunderstandings about learning.

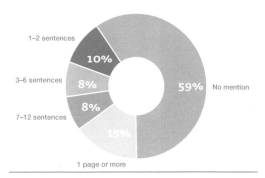

This figure demonstrates the amount of space dedicated to any of the six strategies for effective learning in the 48 teacher-training textbooks commonly used in the US. If every strategy of the six had been mentioned in every textbook, there would be 288 mentions (48 textbooks x 6 strategies) in total. However, most of these mentioned (59 percent) did not exist, and the ones that did tended to be very short. Figure adapted from Pomerance *et al*. (2016).

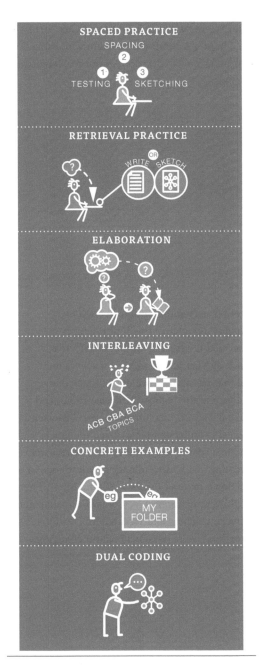

Six strategies for effective learning based on cognitive psychology research.

The National Council on Teacher Quality (NCTQ), which created the Pomerance and colleagues (2016) report, has been in the process of creating teacher training programs that are based on evidence from cognitive research. Other organizations, such as Deans for Impact, have also been vocal about the need for such evidence-based teacher training programs. Unfortunately, programs like that of the NCTQ seem to be few and far between.

IS OUR RESEARCH INACCESSIBLE TO TEACHERS?

The research-to-classroom pipeline is not straightforward. As we've learned over the past two years of engaging in public outreach about learning science, the discrepancy between research and practice in education is a lot more complex than just a communication breakdown.

There are a number of reasons why teachers may not be inclined to engage in "evidence-based practice." For example, Alabama high-school psychology teacher Blake Harvard

The discrepancy between research and practice is a lot more than just a communication breakdown.

(2017) lists three different reasons on his blog "The Effortful Educator": lack of time, lack of access to academic journals, and the difficulty of interpreting technical writing (though interestingly, Laski *et al.* did not find a strong relationship between how difficult teacher educators found cognitive psychological articles, and how (un)likely they were to consult them).

❞ Teachers and students deserve access to this research and time to read through and discuss ways to apply it in the classroom. (2017)

Religious education teacher Dawn Cox in the UK provides some additional suggestions for why teachers may not engage with researchers, including discomfort with change, uncertain findings, and reluctance to accept findings

that disagree with one's intuition (Cox, 2017; see Chapter 3 about the problem with using intuition to make decisions about teaching and learning).

❞ We like to teach in a way that we know, even if it isn't hugely successful; we are reluctant to change. (2017)

Dawn Cox

Another reason that has been cited for teachers' reluctance to adopt practices described in research studies as effective, is a lack of trust in researchers: teachers may feel that researchers are out of touch and unaware of the reality of the classroom, and make irrelevant recommendations. This lack of trust is understandable, given the power dynamic (perceived or otherwise) of researchers "creating" and "disseminating" knowledge in a top-down manner (Gore & Gitlin, 2004). The resulting situation is a lack of two-way dialogue between teachers and researchers – and that's something we're passionate about changing.

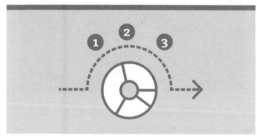

There are a number of reasons why teachers may not be inclined to engage in evidence-based practice.

In top-down communication, the researcher passes on their knowledge. In bi-directional communication, the teacher and the researcher have a conversation and learn from each other.

Teachers face the gargantuan task of integrating information from a myriad of sources in order to best help their students learn. So, we all need to do our part to make sure research is accessible to educators, and that educators are open to research findings. We also need to make it possible for teachers to openly communicate with researchers, so that the most important questions are tackled and, hopefully, answered. That is the main reason we are writing this book: we want to help open up the lines of communication between researchers, teachers, and students. This book is just one of the many ways we are attempting to connect with different groups of people invested in education through our Learning Scientists project. We started this project in January 2016 with the goal of making scientific research on learning more accessible to students, teachers, and other educators. Our outreach efforts so far include a frequently updated blog, downloadable posters and PowerPoints about effective learning strategies in many languages, a podcast, an active social media presence, and many formal and informal collaborations with schools.

In the next chapter, we talk about different types of research evidence about learning, and how it evolves from the lab to the classroom

We want to open up the lines of communication between researchers, teachers, and students.

(Chapter 2). We then go on to talk about why using one's own intuition about how we (and others) learn can be problematic (Chapter 3). Finally, the last chapter of Part 1 deals with pervasive misunderstandings in education, where they come from, and how we might be able to overcome them (Chapter 4).

Whether you are a teacher, a parent, a student, or simply a person interested in how human learning works – there's something for you in this book.

CHAPTER SUMMARY
The goal of cognitive psychologists who are applying their work to the educational domain is to encourage the stakeholders (teachers, students, parents, policy

makers, and more) to do what has been scientifically demonstrated as most effective. Instead, somewhat dubious sources such as untested theories or – even worse – marketing ploys by financially interested parties, create fads in education. The goal of our outreach efforts in general and of this book in particular is to make research from cognitive psychology more accessible to teachers, students, parents, and other educators.

REFERENCES

Abraham, E. P., Chain, E., Fletcher, C. M., Gardner, A. D., Heatley, N. G., Jennings, M. A., & Florey, H. W. (1941). Further observations on penicillin. *The Lancet, 238*(6155), 177–189.

Cox, D. (2017, April). Research in education is great … until you start to try and use it. *missdcoxblog*. Retrieved from https://missdcoxblog.wordpress.com/2017/04/08/research-in-education-is-great-until-you-start-to-try-and-use-it/

Flores, M. E. (n.d.). Teaching & learning styles [Presentation]. Retrieved from www.blinn.edu/twe/radi/Teaching%20%20Learning%20Styles.pdf

Gore, J. M., & Gitlin, A. D. (2004). [Re] Visioning the academic–teacher divide: Power and knowledge in the educational community. *Teachers and Teaching, 10*, 35–58.

Harvard, B. (2017, June). Disconnect in the classroom [Blog post]. *The Effortful Educator*. Retrieved from https://theeffortfuleducator.com/2017/06/04/disconnect-in-the-classroom/

Haynes, R. B., Devereaux, P. J., & Guyatt, G. H. (2002). Physicians' and patients' choices in evidence based practice: Evidence does not make decisions, people do. *BMJ: British Medical Journal, 324*, 1350.

Kerlinger, F. N. (1977). The influence of research on education practice. *Educational Researcher, 6*, 5–12.

Laski, E. V., Reeves, T. D., Ganley, C. M., & Mitchell, R. (2013). Mathematics teacher educators' perceptions and use of cognitive research. *Mind, Brain, and Education, 7*, 63–74.

Ligon, B. L. (2004, January). Penicillin: Its discovery and early development. In *Seminars in Pediatric Infectious Diseases, 15*(1), 52–57.

Pashler, H., McDaniel, M., Rohrer, D., & Bjork, R. (2008). Learning styles: Concepts and evidence. *Psychological Science in the Public Interest, 9*, 105–119.

Pomerance, L., Greenberg, J., & Walsh, K. (2016, January). *Learning about learning: What every teacher needs to know [Report]*. Retrieved from www.nctq.org/dmsView/Learning_About_Learning_Report

Roediger III, H. L. (2013). Applying cognitive psychology to education: Translational educational science. *Psychological Science in the Public Interest, 14*, 1–3.

Rohrer, D., & Pashler, H. (2012). Learning styles: Where's the evidence? *Medical Education, 46*, 34–35.

We are writing this book to tell you what we know about learning from a cognitive perspective.

The quantitative data we rely upon typically include students' performance on various quizzes and assessments.

Experimental manipulations (or randomized controlled trials) are needed in order to get at causal relationships.

The distinction between cognitive psychology and neuroscience is important, but often lost.

Behavioral psychology, cognitive psychology, and neuroscience all come from the experimental discipline.

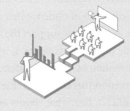

In the lab-to-classroom model, we start at the basic lab level and build up to the classroom.

When research results are communicated, the findings may get distorted.

Evidence can sometimes be contradictory, making it hard to draw conclusions.

Books, blogs, and other media can be helpful, but need to be consumed critically.

DIFFERENT TYPES OF EVIDENCE IN EDUCATION

━━━━

Experimental methods in cognitive psychology allow us to draw causal conclusions about learning. These conclusions need to be communicated carefully to educational stakeholders, so that the findings are not distorted.

What does it mean to be "evidence based" in one's approach to education? After all, there are many different types of evidence that one can use to make decisions, or support the decisions one has already made (see Chapter 3, where we discuss confirmation bias – our tendency to seek out information that supports rather than disproves our beliefs). But, what counts as good evidence? The answer to these questions will depend on your values, your background, and your goals. We are writing this book to tell you what we know about learning from a cognitive perspective.

We are writing this book to tell you what we know about learning from a cognitive perspective.

This knowledge reflects our values (i.e., that learning is important); our backgrounds (as cognitive psychologists who apply their work

to education); and our goals (communicating with teachers and students about the science of learning). After reading this information presented from our perspective, you, the reader, can then add this new perspective to your arsenal of understanding about learning, and integrate the information you find useful into the way you learn or teach.

VARIETIES OF EMPIRICAL EVIDENCE ABOUT HOW WE LEARN

Empirical (that is, data-driven) evidence about how we learn runs the gamut from neuroscientific studies in which individual cells in a rat's brain are stimulated (e.g., Hölscher, Jacob, & Mallot, 2003), to interviews, where descriptions, attitudes, and feelings are gathered from individual teachers or students (Ramey-Gassert, Shroyer, & Staver, 1996). While the former is firmly quantitative (data in the form of numbers are collected) – the latter is mostly qualitative (data in the form of words are collected, though sometimes these data can also be quantified for analyses, creating what's known as a mixed-methods design). In this book, we talk mostly about quantitative data, because those are the data that we tend to collect and analyze. We used the example of single-cell recording in rats earlier in this paragraph, but those are not the type of data we will be talking about in this book. Instead, the quantitative data we rely upon typically include students' performance on various quizzes and assessments, but also students' self-reports about their learning (e.g., we often ask students to predict how well they have learned the material after studying a particular way [Smith, Blunt, Whiffen, & Karpicke, 2016], or how well they think they did on a test [Weinstein & Roediger, 2010]).

The quantitative data we rely upon typically include students' performance on various quizzes and assessments.

That's not to say that we think quantitative data are more important than qualitative data – both are critical to understanding how we can positively impact education. For example, we need interviews and focus groups to understand what kinds of strategies are going to be most feasible in the classroom. But only the more highly controlled experimental research allows us to infer what causes learning.

DESCRIPTIVE AND PREDICTIVE RESEARCH

While each of the vast array of different methods has its own place in the process of understanding learning, experimental manipulations (or randomized controlled trials) are needed in order to get at causal relationships.

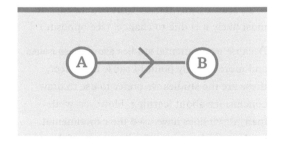

Experimental manipulations (or randomized controlled trials) are needed in order to get at causal relationships.

Cognitive psychologists sometimes use a randomized controlled trial to determine whether something is causing an increase (or decrease) in learning. There are a couple of things researchers must do when running a randomized controlled trial. First, we need to randomly assign students to different groups. This random assignment helps create equivalent groups from the beginning. Second, we need to change something (for example, the type of learning strategy) across the two groups, holding everything else as constant as possible. The key here is to make sure to isolate the thing we are changing, so that it is the only difference between the groups. We also need to make sure at least one of the groups serves as a control group, or a group that serves as a comparison. We need to make sure that the only thing being systematically changed is our manipulation. (Note, sometimes we can systematically manipulate multiple things at once, but these are more complicated designs.) Finally, we then measure learning across the different groups. If we find that our manipulation led to greater learning compared to the control group, and we made sure to conduct the experiment properly with random assignment and appropriate controls, then we can say that our manipulation caused learning. For example, if we randomly assign students to either sleep all night or stay up all night, and those who stay up all night remember less of what they learned the previous day, we can draw the conclusion that lack of sleep hurts learning (see Walker & Stickgold [2004] for a review of this literature). Of course, we won't just stop after one experiment. Evidence from one experiment can support conclusions, but it is when evidence converges from many different studies done in many different contexts that we are comfortable making educational recommendations.

Experiments can also be conducted in a "within-subjects" design. This means that each individual participating in the experiment is serving as their own control. In these experiments, each person participates in all of the conditions. To make sure that the order of conditions or materials are not affecting the results, the researcher randomizes the order of conditions and materials in a process called counterbalancing. The researcher then randomly assigns different participants to different versions of the experiment, with the conditions coming up in different orders. There are a number of ways to implement counterbalancing to maintain control in an experiment so that researchers can identify cause-and-effect relationships. The specifics of how to do this are not important for our purposes here. The important thing to note is that, even when participants are in within-subjects experiments and are participating in multiple learning conditions, in order to determine cause and effect we still need to maintain control and rule out alternate explanations for any findings (e.g., order or material effects).

Experimental studies can be contrasted with correlational studies, from which we can only conclude that learning co-varies with some other factor. Correlational studies involve measuring two or more variables. The researchers can then look at how related two variables are to one another. If two variables are related, or correlated, then we can use one variable to predict the value of another variable. The greater the correlation, the greater accuracy our prediction will have. However, correlations do not allow us to determine causality. When we have a correlation, we cannot determine the direction of a causal relationship, and there could also be another variable that is causing both of the study variables to be related.

For example, in a study about sleep and academic achievement in medical students, sleep quality during the semester was correlated with medical board exam grades (Ahrberg, Dresler, Niedermaier, Steiger, & Genzel, 2012). One might conclude that the poor sleep quality is causing lower grades, but there are other possible interpretations. For example, the direction of the causal relationship could be different from what we think. Perhaps having better grades might cause students to relax and sleep better, while poor grades might cause students to be anxious and unable to sleep. There could also be a third variable such as genetics causing both sleep disturbances and poor academic performance. The possibilities are endless, and the correlation does not tell us about the causal nature of the relationship between sleep and academic performance.

Another problem with correlational studies is that sometimes completely unrelated variables can be correlated just by chance. There is a fun website called Spurious Correlations (www.tylervigen.com/ and now also a book; Vigen, 2015) where the creator graphs all sorts of random pairs of variables that happen to produce a correlation. For example, this graph shows ten-year trends for per capita consumption of cheese and the numbers of lawyers in Hawaii. Perhaps you can think of some reasons why those might be related, but most likely it is due to chance! (see opposite)

Because experimental studies avoid these issues and more directly point to cause and effect, those are the studies we prefer to use to draw conclusions about learning. However, while many disciplines have used the experimental method, we focus specifically on one of them: cognitive psychology.

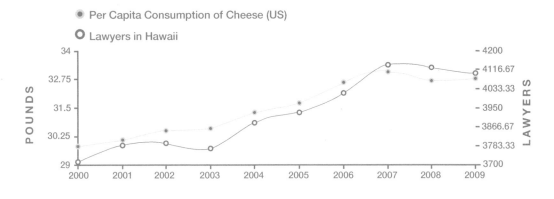

Per Capita Consumption of Cheese (US) Correlates with Lawyers in Hawaii

Correlation: 98%. Sources: USDA & ABA tyervigen.com

The spurious correlation between per capita consumption of cheese and the numbers of lawyers in Hawaii. Data from Vigen (2015).

BRAIN, MIND, AND BEHAVIOR

In this book, we focus mainly on findings from cognitive psychology. However, research from this field is sometimes confused with neuroscience, at least in the mainstream media where findings from cognitive psychology are reported with the word "neuroscience" in the title (e.g., see the blog post from StaffWriters at OnlineUniversities. com [2012], which includes many references to "neuroscience" when they are actually referring to findings from cognitive psychology).

The distinction between cognitive psychology and neuroscience is important, but often lost.

A very simple explanation of the differences between cognitive psychology and neuroscience is that cognitive psychology focuses on explanations related to the mind, whereas neuroscience is concerned with figuring out what happens in the brain. For example, cognitive psychologists discuss abstract processes such as encoding, storage, and retrieval when talking about memory and trying to explain why we forget or remember. Neuroscientists, on the other hand, are concerned with pin-pointing those processes in terms of physical activity in the brain, often on quite a detailed level. We feel that cognitive psychology is currently a better knowledge base for teachers and learners from which to extrapolate findings that are applicable to the classroom, because this approach has a longer history from which to draw conclusions, and also because it provides more of an overview of how we learn rather than a very detailed understanding of what that looks like in the brain.

About 20 years ago, an article called "Education and the brain: A bridge too far"

(Bruer, 1997) was published. The author argued that findings about the brain were being misapplied to education, with simplifications and misunderstandings of the actual science. We talk more about these misunderstandings in Chapter 4. Bruer suggested that for now we should focus on bridging the gap between cognition and education (the goal of this book!), as well as the gap between cognition and neuroscience. That is, while we know a lot about cognitive processes and a lot about how the brain functions, the two fields are still relatively separate, with insufficient understanding of how cognitive processes map onto the brain.

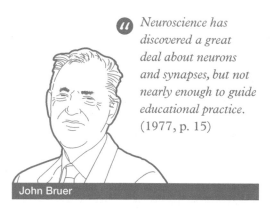

> *Neuroscience has discovered a great deal about neurons and synapses, but not nearly enough to guide educational practice.* (1977, p. 15)

John Bruer

This was true 20 years ago, and was true eight years ago when we wrote a chapter in a book called *Neuroscience in Education: The Good, the Bad, and the Ugly* (Roediger, Finn, & Weinstein, 2012), and it is still true today (e.g., see Smeyers [2016] for a similar argument). Having said that, valiant attempts are being made to connect the two fields (Hardt, Einarsson, & Nader, 2010), and there are some basics of memory at the neural level that are useful to understand, which you will find in Chapter 7. You can also read about a more optimistic outlook on the future role of neuroscience in education in a piece by Daniel Ansari and colleagues (Ansari, Coch, & De Smedt, 2011).

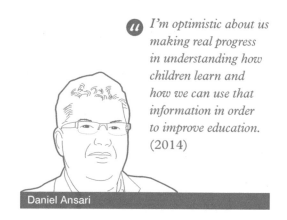

> *I'm optimistic about us making real progress in understanding how children learn and how we can use that information in order to improve education.* (2014)

Daniel Ansari

Since we haven't yet discovered a way to measure mental processes directly, what we do instead is try to observe and measure behavior, and then infer the mental processes from the behavior that we've been able to observe and measure. In fact, the field of cognitive psychology evolved directly from behaviorism, in which behavior is observed and measured *without* cognitive explanations.

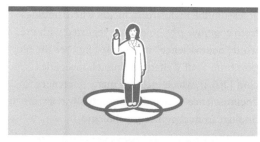

Behavioral psychology, cognitive psychology, and neuroscience all come from the experimental discipline.

Since both cognitive psychology and behaviorism measure behavior (e.g., performance on tests), behavioral studies often converge with cognitive studies in terms of recommendations for teaching and learning (see Markovits & Weinstein, [2018], for a review). Behavioral psychology, cognitive psychology, and neuroscience all come from the experimental discipline. We, however, prefer the cognitive approach because it not only provides us with information about what works, but also helps us figure out how and why certain learning strategies work better than others.

THE LAB TO CLASSROOM MODEL

A very important aspect of this process is what we like to call the lab-to-classroom model. A misunderstanding of our discipline could lead one to believe that all cognitive researchers carry out their work in the lab (Black, n.d.). While this is not true, it would be accurate to state that we begin our research in the lab. In what we call the "basic lab level," participants take part in very simplified tasks, studying very simplified material.

That is, participants might be learning lists of unrelated words, or even nonsense syllables. These materials are highly controlled, and often not much like something you or I might actually want to learn in real life. The context

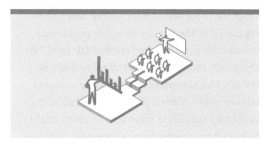

In the lab-to-classroom model, we start at the basic lab level and build up to the classroom.

in which the research takes place may also be quite contrived and unrealistic. But the benefits of starting at this level are that we have much more control over the participants' learning environment. This control allows us to hone in on what factors are actually causing (or preventing) learning.

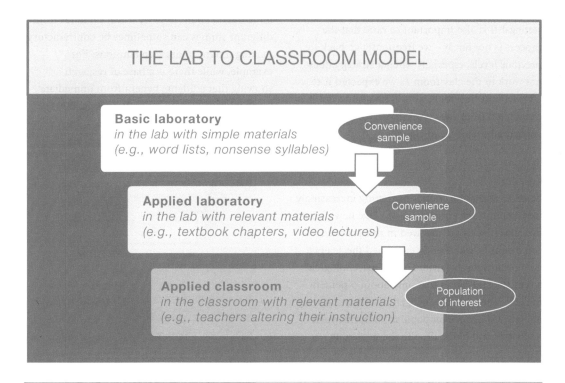

THE LAB TO CLASSROOM MODEL

Basic laboratory
*in the lab with simple materials
(e.g., word lists, nonsense syllables)*

Convenience sample

Applied laboratory
*in the lab with relevant materials
(e.g., textbook chapters, video lectures)*

Convenience sample

Applied classroom
*in the classroom with relevant materials
(e.g., teachers altering their instruction)*

Population of interest

Once we come across a technique that can be replicated in the lab, the research progresses to something we call the "applied lab level." At this point, the experiment still takes place in the lab, but now participants will be studying educationally relevant materials instead of the artificially simplified materials. So, they might be reading a chapter from a textbook, watching a lecture, etc. And, once we find that the strategy we examined at the basic lab level works here as well, it is now time to continue onto the classroom level. At this stage, we will actually go into schools, with realistic material, and examine the effectiveness of learning techniques in this realistic context, usually with the help of the teachers.

The reason why we take so long to get to the applied classroom level is that this stage is costly, both in terms of money and, most importantly, in terms of time. We certainly do not want to be wasting teacher and student time with activities and techniques that haven't been shown to work effectively in the basic and applied laboratory settings! It is also important to note that the process is not linear – we frequently go back to previous levels, especially when a strategy does not work in the classroom as we expected it to. Throughout this book, we will be using examples of research from each level (basic laboratory, applied laboratory, and classroom).

COMMUNICATING THE SCIENCE OF LEARNING

Science communication is becoming increasingly important in the current age of "fake news," but not all scientists are involved in this practice. For example, we recently examined the science communication behaviors of 327 psychological scientists, and found that only about 5 percent of them were actively engaged in communicating about their science on popular platforms such as Twitter and blogs, despite the negligible

financial burden of these activities (Weinstein & Sumeracki, 2017).

This is a problem, because if we – scientists – are not doing the communication ourselves, the results of our research risk getting distorted as they make their way through to teachers and learners.

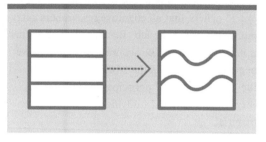

When research results are communicated, the findings may get distorted.

Moreover, no one study can give us definitive information about how we learn; evidence from different studies can sometimes be contradictory, making it hard to draw conclusions. For example, while there is a base of research showing that students benefit from immediate feedback (Epstein, Epstein, & Brosvic, 2001),

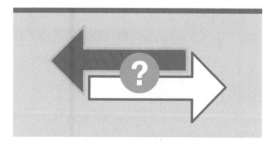

Evidence can sometimes be contradictory, making it hard to draw conclusions.

more recent research suggests that delaying feedback could be more helpful in some situations (Butler, Karpicke, & Roediger, 2007).

The process goes as follows: data are collected and written up by scientists. Eventually, the write-up of the data is accepted for publication in a peer-reviewed academic journal. After publication, the paper may be picked up by mainstream media, and then people will pass their impression of the media coverage along to other people. Unfortunately, however, the media coverage may have introduced errors or misunderstandings into their interpretation of the science (see Chapter 4), and these errors can be further exacerbated through word of mouth.

As such, and as we already mentioned in Chapter 1, we believe that it is very important for us as scientists to keep communicating about our research findings. Of course, books, blogs, and even the media can be helpful, but all need to be consumed critically.

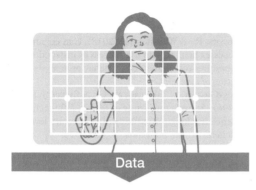
Data

Journal publication

Media

Word of mouth

Books, blogs, and other media can be helpful, but need to be consumed critically.

In this book, we cite a variety of sources, ranging from academic journal articles to blog posts. However, where we cite blog posts, we have checked to make sure that they are describing the research accurately. When you are reading other pieces, you might want to ask yourself: are the authors of these works reading and interpreting or maybe even conducting the research itself – for example, as is the case in the book "Make It Stick" by Brown, Roediger, and McDaniel (2014) – or are they relying on secondary sources (such as other books and blogs!) to draw conclusions? And, always stay alert for overextensions and misunderstandings, such as those we discuss in Chapter 4.

CHAPTER SUMMARY

A large number of disciplines contribute to our understanding of how we learn. We focus specifically on cognitive psychology, which is an experimental discipline and thus provides the strongest evidence for causal conclusions (that is, predicting rather than merely describing). In our discipline, we start by running experiments in a lab (known as basic research), and then increase the relevance of the materials and settings involved in the study (applied research), eventually taking our research to the classroom. But, our job does not stop there – we need to also communicate the research findings beyond academia, in order to help prevent and resolve misunderstandings and misinterpretations.

REFERENCES

Ahrberg, K., Dresler, M., Niedermaier, S., Steiger, A., & Genzel, L. (2012). The interaction between sleep quality and academic performance. *Journal of Psychiatric Research, 46*, 1618–1622.

Ansari, D. (2014). Daniel Ansari – The Science Network Interview [YouTube video]. Retrieved from https://youtu.be/vvLsQ29RQtg

Ansari, D., Coch, D., & De Smedt, B. (2011). Connecting education and cognitive neuroscience: Where will the journey take us? *Educational Philosophy and Theory, 43*, 37–42.

Black, C. (n.d.). Science/fiction: How learning styles became a myth. Retrieved from http://carolblack.org/science-fiction/

Brown, P. C., Roediger, H. L., & McDaniel, M. A. (2014). *Make It Stick. The Science of Successful Learning.* Cambridge, MA: Harvard University Press.

Bruer, J. T. (1997). Education and the brain: A bridge too far. *Educational Researcher, 26*, 4–16.

Butler, A. C., Karpicke, J. D., & Roediger III, H. L. (2007). The effect of type and timing of feedback on learning from multiple-choice tests. *Journal of Experimental Psychology: Applied, 13*, 273–281.

Epstein, M. L., Epstein, B. B., & Brosvic, G. M. (2001). Immediate feedback during academic testing. *Psychological Reports, 88*, 889–894.

Hardt, O., Einarsson, E. Ö., & Nader, K. (2010). A bridge over troubled water: Reconsolidation as a link between cognitive and neuroscientific memory research traditions. *Annual Review of Psychology, 61*, 141–167.

Hölscher, C., Jacob, W., & Mallot, H. A. (2003). Reward modulates neuronal activity in the hippocampus of the rat. *Behavioural Brain Research, 142*, 181–191.

Markovits, R., & Weinstein, Y. (2018). Can cognitive processes help explain the success of instructional techniques recommended by behavior analysts? *npj Science of Learning.*

Ramey-Gassert, L., Shroyer, M. G., & Staver, J. R. (1996). A qualitative study of factors influencing science teaching self-efficacy of elementary level teachers. *Science Education, 80*, 283–315.

Roediger, H. L., Finn, B., & Weinstein, Y. (2012). Improving metacognition to enhance educational practice. In S. Della Sala & M. Anderson (Eds.), *Neuroscience in education: The good, the bad, and the ugly* (pp. 128–151). Oxford: Oxford University Press.

Smeyers, P. (2016). Neurophilia: Guiding educational research and the educational field? *Journal of Philosophy of Education, 50*, 62–75.

Smith, M. A., Blunt, J. R., Whiffen, J. W., & Karpicke, J. D. (2016). Does providing prompts during retrieval practice improve learning? *Applied Cognitive Psychology, 30*, 544–553.

Staff Writers (2012). 9 signs that neuroscience has entered the classroom. *OnineUniversities.com.* Retrieved from www.onlineuniversities.com/blog/2012/06/9-signs-that-neuroscience-has-entered-classroom/

Vigen, T. (2015). *Spurious correlations.* Hachette Books.

Walker, M. P., & Stickgold, R. (2004). Sleep-dependent learning and memory consolidation. *Neuron, 44*, 121–133.

Weinstein, Y., & Roediger, H. L. (2010). Retrospective bias in test performance: Providing easy items at the beginning of a test makes students believe they did better on it. *Memory & Cognition, 38*, 366–376.

Weinstein, Y., & Sumeracki, M. A. (2017). Are Twitter and blogs important tools for the modern psychological scientist? *Perspectives on Psychological Science, 12*, 1171–1175.

Our own intuitions as to how we learn and how we should teach are not always correct.

Our intuitions can lead us to pick the wrong learning strategies.

Once we land on a learning strategy, we tend to seek out evidence that favors the strategy.

College students tend to read their textbook and notes repeatedly as a learning strategy, because it feels good.

Reading repeatedly takes extra time, but is less effective than retrieving information.

When students practice retrieving information, they predict poorer performance because it feels hard.

People are more likely to look at confirmatory than contradictory evidence when examining their beliefs.

The problem with faulty intuitions and biases is that they are notoriously difficult to correct.

Science acknowledges human bias, and constantly tries to combat it.

IS INTUITION THE ENEMY OF TEACHING AND LEARNING?

Our own intuitions as to how we learn and how we should teach are not always correct, and can lead us to pick the wrong learning strategies. The problem with these faulty intuitions and biases is that they are notoriously difficult to correct.

The idea of relying on personal intuition versus expertise has long been debated in medicine. For example, much concern surrounds the use of vaccines, with one intuitive argument being that it is bad to put "chemicals" in the body (the counterargument, of course, is that even water is technically a "chemical"). Thankfully, for the most part, scientific expertise is winning the battle against intuition with regards to vacation: for example, well over 90 percent of children in the US and the UK (where Megan and Yana grew up, respectively) are up to date with their measles, mumps, and rubella vaccine by their second birthday (CDC, 2017; NHS, 2017).

When it comes to education, however, we seem to be much less inclined to turn to experts. In particular, there seems to be a huge distrust of any information that comes "from above." Instead, there's a preference for relying on our intuitions – be it teachers', parents', or students' – about what's best for learning.

One source of this tendency is that virtually every one of us has years of experience as a student, which leads us to trust our own intuitions more than we should. For example, in the UK and the US, 81 percent and 90 percent respectively of 25–64-year-olds have attained at least a secondary education (OECD, 2017), which means a majority of the citizens in these two countries have at least 13 years of experience in education. Further, becoming a primary or secondary teacher requires a bachelor's degree; so, teachers are likely to have 17 years of experience as a student before entering a classroom, and we can hardly blame them for using this experience to inform their teaching practice.

Our own intuitions as to how we learn and how we should teach are not always correct.

Of course, experience as a student (and later, as a teacher) can be very valuable in building a teaching philosophy and practice. Unfortunately, however, our own intuitions as to how we learn and how we should teach are not always correct.

Moreover, the way we were taught in school may not be the best or most efficient way to learn. And despite being seasoned students, our intuitions about how much we have learned on a topic can often be misleading, too.

There are two major problems that arise from a reliance on intuition. The first is that our intuitions can lead us to pick the wrong learning strategies.

Our intuitions can lead us to pick the wrong learning strategies.

Second, once we land on a learning strategy, we tend to seek out "evidence" that favors the strategy we have picked, while ignoring evidence that refutes our intuitions (i.e., confirmation bias, which we discuss later on in this chapter).

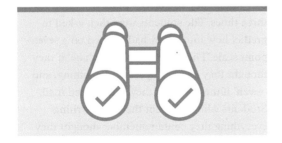

Once we land on a learning strategy, we tend to seek out evidence that favors the strategy.

The first problem with intuition is evidenced by the frequent survey finding that college students tend to read their textbook and notes repeatedly as a learning strategy. In fact, one survey conducted at Washington University in St. Louis – a top university in the US – revealed that 55 percent of students utilize repeated reading as their number-one study strategy (Karpicke, Butler, & Roediger, 2009). Yet research indicates that repeated reading is not the best way to learn.

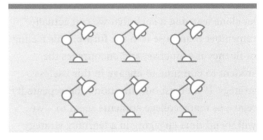

College students tend to read their textbook and notes repeatedly as a learning strategy, because it feels good.

There are many studies comparing what happens when students read portions of a textbook once, to what happens when students read those same textbook sections twice in a row. These experiments use a variety of different topics from textbooks, a variety of different types of learning assessments, and various delays from when the students read to when learning is assessed. Results from these studies overwhelmingly show that reading the textbook twice in a row takes extra time, but does not improve long-term retention of the information (Callendar & McDaniel, 2009).

But re-reading feels good. The more we read a passage, the more fluently we are able to read it. However, reading fluency does not mean we're engaging with the information on a deep level,

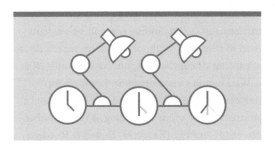

Reading repeatedly takes extra time, but is less effective than retrieving information.

let alone learning it such that we can actually remember it and use it in the future. This feeling of fluency is seductive, and encourages the student to continue to engage in this useless strategy. If we trust our intuitions and repeatedly read – as many college students seem to – we will spend time engaging in a learning strategy that simply does not work in most cases, and certainly does not improve learning in the long run.

The finding that repeated reading does not improve learning may be surprising to you. Many of us have had the experience of reading

something twice, and feeling that we are "getting more out of it" the second time. Yet our predictions about how much we are learning are not accurate. When college students are asked to predict how much they think they are learning from repeated reading, many are extremely overconfident (Roediger & Karpicke, 2006). On the other hand, predictions made after engaging in more effective strategies – like answering practice questions or writing down everything you know about a topic – tend to be too low.

When students practice retrieving information, they predict poorer performance because it feels hard.

Roediger and Karpicke provide a striking example. Students learned a small section of a textbook by either reading four times or by reading once and then trying to write down everything they could remember from that text three times. The students were then asked to predict how much they had learned on a seven-point scale. They should have said 'one' if they thought they had hardly learned anything, and 'seven' if they thought they had learned it all. Students who had spent their time writing everything they could remember thought they had learned less than the students who spent their time reading and re-reading.

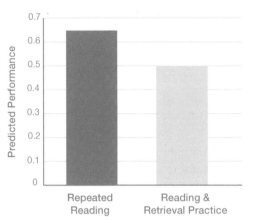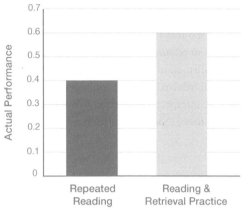

This graph shows predicted and actual learning after retrieval practice and re-reading. Data from Roediger & Karpicke (2006).

Then, one week later, the students took a learning assessment where they again had to write down everything they could remember, and got points for every piece of correct information that they wrote down. The students who practiced writing everything they knew during the first session could remember more of the information a week later than the students who read and re-read. Compare this performance to the predictions students made, and you will see a virtually mirror-like effect between predicted learning and actual learning. In other words, students' intuitions led them to make faulty predictions about their learning. (See Chapter 10 for more about this experiment, and more about this effective study strategy.)

As college professors, we have seen this illusion baffle students. Occasionally students will come to see one of us in our offices – usually the students who often miss class and have not heard the spiel on effective learning strategies – and say they are unhappy with their performance in the class, and that they thought they aced a recent exam on which they actually scored quite

poorly. We ask them how they prepared for the exam, and they almost always tell us they "read the textbook and looked over all the notes." They also often add that they "spent tons of time studying."

At this point, we sit them down and remind them (or tell them for the first time, if they missed it) about the benefits of practicing retrieval for learning, and ask them to try it out. This is often met with much resistance – retrieval practice isn't easy – but those who do try it are usually pleased with the results (Wallis & Morris, 2016).

We just saw how our intuitions aren't always accurate when it comes to our learning, or the learning of our students. The second big problem arising from reliance on intuition is confirmation bias. Confirmation bias is the tendency for us to search out information that confirms our own beliefs, or interpret information in a way that confirms them (Nickerson, 1998).

People are more likely to look at confirmatory than contradictory evidence when examining their beliefs.

We make biased choices, then seek out evidence to confirm them.

How does this affect instruction and learning? Well, once we adopt a belief about what produces a lot of learning, we tend to look for examples that confirm our belief. So, imagine that you're a firm believer in learning styles

because you feel like you've experienced improvement in your students when you adapt your teaching to their learning style. Then a party-pooper like us comes along, and tells you that matching instruction to preferred learning styles is actually not helpful for learning (as we did already in Chapter 1, and do again in Chapter 4). You decide to see for yourself whether what they're saying is true. What would you Google: "evidence for learning styles" or "evidence against learning styles"?

Although no study to our knowledge has directly tested the above research question (although it

| A belief | Evidence against | Evidence for |

now sounds quite interesting to us!), research from other domains suggests that people are more likely to look at confirmatory than contradictory evidence.

For example, in one study conducted in the run up to the 2008 US elections, participants browsed a specially designed online magazine. Their behavior was recorded in terms of which articles they chose to read on topics such as abortion, health care, gun ownership, and the minimum wage, and also how long they spent on each article. When given freedom to explore the magazine, participants generally clicked more and looked longer at political messages that were consistent with their own beliefs. For example, those against abortion were more likely to click on an article titled "cruelty of prochoice," whereas those in favor were more likely to click on "abortion is prolife." (We should note that there were some fascinating interactions with other variables such as partisanship and level of news consumption that are beyond the scope of this chapter; Knobloch-Westerwick & Kleinman, 2012).

If we believe in something, we are also more likely to notice and remember examples that support our belief than to notice and remember examples that do not. So, if we believe in learning styles, we are also more likely to notice times when we think we see learning styles working, and forget about the times when it doesn't appear to work. For example, when Johnny doesn't get your verbal description, but finally he has a lightbulb moment when you show him a diagram, we think, "Ah ha! There it is!" In reality, was it learning styles? Or just that he got a second presentation in a different format? What if the two were reversed? What about times when a diagram isn't as helpful?

The problem with faulty intuitions and biases is that they are notoriously difficult to correct (Pasquinelli, 2012). Instructing people that

these biases exist has limited success (Fischhoff, 1982). Somewhat more effective is a "consider-the-opposite" exercise, where people are asked to list reasons for why their opinion might not be true, before seeking out additional information on the topic (Mussweiler, Strack, & Pfeiffer, 2000). We're curious to know – how often do teachers have an intuition about how students are learning in the classroom, then sit down to write out the reasons why they may be wrong? It might be an interesting exercise to try.

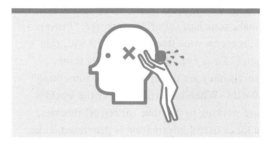

The problem with faulty intuitions and biases is that they are notoriously difficult to correct.

And by the way, just because we research and teach about these biases, doesn't mean we're immune to them, either! Take the story about the students who come to our offices from earlier in this chapter – it may be that we're conveniently forgetting all those other students who came to us complaining that they'd failed after diligently following instructions to practice retrieval. Does conceding this point reveal us to be rampant hypocrites? Not really, we hope. Instead, we hope that there's a way to acknowledge that we're all humans who go about our daily business making imperfect choices and judgments.

The goal of science is to try to disprove ideas, not prove them. In fact, whenever we see the word "prove," we immediately become skeptical. (Think, "This shampoo is proven to

Science acknowledges human bias, and constantly tries to combat it.

null hypothesis (that a given strategy produces no more learning than a control) and evidence from many different groups of students and in many different situations continues to support the notion that the learning strategy produces learning? Now we can be far more confident! If we can all agree to start acknowledging our human flaws and mindfully look for evidence that has been generated rather than relying upon intuition, maybe we'd help more students actually learn rather than get seduced by something that feels like learning but isn't at all.

make your hair softer!" – or worse, "Proven success on your standardized test with this app!" Does everyone immediately think, surely, they are just trying to sell something? We do.) When scientists all over the world are working to disprove (or reject) theories, a lot of useful information is generated. Take learning styles, which has been disproven many, many times (see Chapter 4 for more on this misunderstanding). That's a concept we can safely say is not worth our time and money. But when scientists keep testing the

CHAPTER SUMMARY

The idea of relying on personal intuition versus expertise has long been debated in medicine, but thankfully, scientific expertise seems to be winning the battle in many cases. Unfortunately, this is largely not the case in education. Instead, there is a preference for relying on our intuitions – be it teachers', parents', or students'– about what's best for learning. But relying on intuition may be a bad idea for teachers and learners alike. Going against our intuitions to embrace findings research can be hard, but could help us improve our teaching and learning practices.

Here are the data. What conclusion can we draw from them?

Here's the conclusion. What data can we find to support it?

REFERENCES

Callendar, A. A., & McDaniel, M. A. (2009). The limited benefits of rereading educational texts. *Contemporary Educational Psychology, 34,* 30–41.

CDC (2017). *Immunization.* Retrieved from www.cdc.gov/nchs/fastats/immunize.htm

Fischhoff, B. (1982). Debiasing. In D. Kahneman, P. Slovic, & A. Tversky (Eds.), *Judgment under uncertainty: Heuristics and biases.* Cambridge: Cambridge University Press, 422–444.

Karpicke, J. D., Butler, A. C., & Roediger, H. L. (2009). Metacognitive strategies in student learning: Do students practice retrieval when they study on their own? *Memory, 17,* 471–479.

Knobloch-Westerwick, S., & Kleinman, S. B. (2012). Preelection selective exposure confirmation bias versus informational utility. *Communication Research, 39,* 170–193.

Mussweiler, T., Strack, F., & Pfeiffer, T. (2000). Overcoming the inevitable anchoring effect: Considering the opposite compensates for selective accessibility. *Personality and Social Psychology Bulletin, 26,* 1142–1150.

NHS (2017). Childhood vaccination coverage statistics, England, 2016–17. Retrieved from https://digital.nhs.uk/catalogue/PUB30085

Nickerson, R. S. (1998). Confirmation bias: A ubiquitous phenomenon in many guises. *Review of General Psychology, 2,* 175–220.

OECD (2017). *Education at a glance 2017: OECD indicators.* Paris: OECD Publishing. http://dx.doi.org/10.1787/eag-2017-en

Pasquinelli, E. (2012). Neuromyths: Why do they exist and persist? *Mind, Brain, and Education, 6,* 89–96.

Roediger, H. L., & Karpicke, J. D. (2006). Test-enhanced learning: Taking memory tests improves long-term retention. *Psychological Science, 17,* 249–255.

Wallis, C., & Morris, R. (2016, January). *Study tips and tricks* [Blog post]. Retrieved from https://syntheticduo.wordpress.com/2016/01/19/study-tips-and-tricks/

PERVASIVE MISUNDERSTANDINGS ABOUT LEARNING

Scientists are trying to understand in detail how learning occurs in the brain.

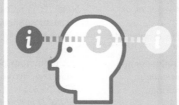

Overall, educators are highly enthusiastic about what cognitive psychology and neuroscience have to offer education.

The problem arises when information about learning is taken out of context and condensed into overgeneralizations.

We may put children in visually noisy learning environments because we misunderstand their need for stimulation.

A lot of people hold on to the idea that learning styles are important and meaningful.

Just because some tasks require more resources from one hemisphere, does not mean individuals differ in terms of their brains.

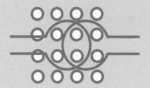

The relationship between interest in neuroscience and accurate understanding of learning is complex.

In some cases, those most interested in neuroscience can be more susceptible to believing incorrect information.

Shaming people for their beliefs is not an effective way to change minds.

PERVASIVE MISUNDERSTANDINGS ABOUT LEARNING

How they arise, and what we can do

Misunderstandings about scientific findings can be the result of an honest desire to learn. Attempts at correcting misunderstandings can backfire, strengthening inaccurate beliefs.

Based on various scientific disciplines (see Chapter 2), there's a lot we know about learning, and there's also a great deal we don't know. But who is the "we" in that statement? If a small, select group of scientists understand some process – say, the chemical reaction that occurs when neutrons collide – does that count as "known"? Or does it need to become part of everyday knowledge, such as the fact that the Earth is round? Scientists found this out, but now the average person also knows that the Earth is round – whereas in the neutron collision example, only a select few know the information. These two examples come from physics, but the same parallel can be drawn in learning: a small select group of scientists are trying to understand in detail how learning occurs in the brain, but all of us know that children are not innately equipped with knowledge about the world and need to be taught.

This is ok. We don't all need to know exactly how synapses operate in the brain; but what about a more general understanding of the mind? Isn't it useful to know that as soon as we encounter a piece of information, we immediately start to forget it? Or what about the fact that our memories are not like libraries, but instead reconstruct everything we try to retrieve? (For more about memory, see Chapter 7.) We think that type of information is useful – and on the whole, so do teachers. A survey of teachers around the world revealed that, overall, educators are highly enthusiastic about what cognitive psychology and neuroscience have to offer to education (Pickering & Howard-Jones, 2007).

Scientists are trying to understand in detail how learning occurs in the brain.

Overall, educators are highly enthusiastic about what cognitive psychology and neuroscience have to offer education.

The problem arises when information about learning – particularly about how learning occurs in the brain – is taken out of context and condensed into simplified overgeneralizations.

The problem arises when information about learning is taken out of context and condensed into overgeneralizations.

referring to them as "misunderstandings" or "misconceptions."

> *"* *Misconceptions are beliefs that contradict the current state of scientific evidence.* (2017)

Annette Taylor

Once the message is passed down through various channels (from researchers, to journalists, to professional development workshops, to teachers), the science behind the "fact" often is lost, and the conclusion distorted.

Eventually, what started as a simplification or overgeneralization can turn into a slogan – and an inaccurate one at that. Indeed, a common term used to describe misunderstandings about the brain is "neuromyths." However, myths about learning and the brain typically start from a grain of truth, large or small. For this reason, we would rather not call them "myths," instead

What are the most common misunderstandings? Two students in Yana's lab, Marcus and Shannon, sifted through 12 empirical papers that surveyed a total of 14,737 participants in 15 different countries, to determine which misunderstandings were most commonly believed across the world.

In the table opposite, you will see the ten most common misunderstandings about learning and the brain, along with the average percentage of study participants who believed each one.

Now, let's dig into three of these misunderstandings.

Rank	Misunderstanding	% who believe it
1	Individuals learn better when they receive information in their preferred learning style (e.g., auditory, visual, kinesthetic)	93%
2	Environments that are rich in stimuli improve the brains of pre-school children	89%
3	Short bouts of coordination exercises can improve integration of left and right hemisphere brain function	76%
4	Exercises that rehearse coordination of motor-perception skills can improve literacy skills	74%
5	Differences in hemispheric dominance (left brain, right brain) can help explain individual differences among learners.	74%
6	It has been scientifically proven that fatty acid supplements (omega-3 and omega-6) have a positive effect on academic achievement	61%
7	Emotional brain processes interrupt those brain processes involved with reasoning	60%
8	We only use 10% of our brain	49%
9	Memory is stored in the brain much like as in a computer: each memory goes into a tiny piece of the brain	48%
10	Children are less attentive after consuming sugary drinks and/or snacks	47%

The data in this table have been aggregated from the following studies: Deligiannidi and Howard-Jones (2015); Dekker, Lee, Howard-Jones, and Jolles (2012); Dündar and Gündüz (2016); Ferrero, Garaiza, and Vadillo (2016); Gleichgerrcht, Luttges, Salvarezza, and Campos (2015); Herculano-Houzel (2002); Hermida, Segretin, Soni García, and Lipina (2016); Macdonald, Germine, Anderson, Christodoulou, and McGrath (2017); Karakus, Howard-Jones, and Jay (2015); Papadatou-Pastou, Haliou, and Vlachos, (2017); and Pei, Howard-Jones, Zhang, Liu, & Jin (2015). Note that not all of the studies mentioned included each statement.

Shannon Rowley & Marcus Lithander

1) "ENVIRONMENTS THAT ARE RICH IN STIMULI IMPROVE THE BRAINS OF PRE-SCHOOL CHILDREN"

This belief describes the idea that young children should be exposed to many interesting things to see and explore, and often manifests itself as gaudy, "visually noisy" classrooms (Erickson, 2017).

Some of our everyday understanding about enriching environments may come from a misapplication of studies performed in other species (e.g., rats). A study from the 1960s found that rats deprived of stimulation had sparser connections between their neurons, and by word-of-mouth this could have led people to believe that humans needed an "enriched" environment in order to thrive (Diamond, Krech, & Rosenzweig, 1964). It is also possible that this belief stems from an overcorrection for the real findings that sensory deprivation leads to decreased learning (Vernon & Hoffman, 1956). However, true sensory deprivation is very extreme, and would involve putting a child in a situation where they cannot see, hear, or feel *anything*. Take the classic case study of Genie as an example of extreme isolation (Fromkin, Krashen, Curtiss, Rigler, &

Rigler, 1974). Genie was found in 1970, when she was 13 years old. She had been locked in a room by herself by her father, and was completely socially isolated. She spent much of her time tied to her crib or to a toilet chair. When child welfare found her, she could not talk. This is an extreme case of sensory deprivation, but demonstrates the type of deprivation that actually leads to a lack of development.

The reality is that in their everyday lives, even without decorated classrooms, children encounter sufficient information to enable their brains to develop normally. In fact, overly decorated classrooms can actually lead to a decrease in learning relative to more sparsely decorated classrooms, due to potential for distraction (Fisher, Godwin, & Seltman, 2014). Colorful decorations can lead children to shift or split their attention away from the teacher and the current learning tasks, and this can interfere with learning (see Chapter 6 on attention).

We may put children in visually noisy learning environments because we misunderstand their need for stimulation.

2) "INDIVIDUALS LEARN BETTER WHEN THEY RECEIVE INFORMATION IN THEIR PREFERRED LEARNING STYLE (E.G., AUDITORY, VISUAL, KINESTHETIC)"

There is currently no solid evidence from controlled experiments to suggest that teaching in someone's preferred modality (e.g., auditory)

will help them learn. And yet, a lot of people hold on to the idea that learning styles are important and meaningful. Where does this misunderstanding come from?

A lot of people hold on to the idea that learning styles are important and meaningful.

It's likely that the idea comes from an obvious truth: that individuals have *preferences* about the way they study. This is non-controversial; it would be strange to deny the existence of preferences, since we all have them. But where the overextension happens is where people immediately assume that these preferences should be honored in order to maximize learning. Think of the following nutritional analogy: let's say one person likes apples, while the other person likes carrots.

Now let's imagine we measure out 100 calories' worth of apples and carrots, and have these two people eat either their preferred food, or their nonpreferred food, on top of what they normally eat, every day for a month. We then measure how much weight they gained (assuming they were maintaining their weight with their own caloric intake). Will they put on a different amount of weight depending on whether they ate their preferred or nonpreferred food? No. They are taking in the same number of calories regardless of whether they like or dislike the food. At the same time, carrots and apples contain different nutrients, so ideally, people would be eating a mix of both!

Learning styles seem impossible to get away from. Indeed, surveys conducted across the world typically find that over 90 percent of teachers believe in adapting teaching to each student's preferred learning style. This statistic in and of itself might not be surprising, but the more surprising result is that greater interest in the neuroscience of education tends to be related to stronger – rather than weaker – beliefs in learning styles (Dekker *et al.*, 2012)! Why is this the case? A review of the literature (Newton, 2015) suggests that one factor may be the proliferation of research that uses learning styles questionnaires and then concludes that learning styles are important and useful (without actually demonstrating this in a scientifically sound manner). Any well-meaning teacher who searches the literature is thus going to find many positive references to learning styles. Having said that, another survey did find that taking multiple classes about neuroscience reduced the belief in this idea, which is at least somewhat reassuring (Macdonald *et al.*, 2017).

The thing is, the explanation for why we can't conclude that learning styles are useful based on any of the published data is actually quite nuanced (Pashler, McDaniel, Rohrer, & Bjork, 2009). In order to understand why learning styles aren't useful, teachers would need to invest quite a lot of time in understanding the research methods involved in the studies that claim to demonstrate their usefulness. So, what we need is more open-access, clear explanations of the research. These can include more traditional academic articles (Kirschner, 2017), but also popular science materials such as videos (https://ssec.si.edu/sending-learning-styles-out-style) and blog posts (www.learningscientists.org/blog/2017/5/25-1).

The most ironic thing about learning styles is that even if learning styles *did* matter for learning, a better idea would be to teach to students' nonpreferred styles, in order to strengthen their weaknesses.

3) "SOME OF US ARE 'LEFT-BRAINED' AND SOME ARE 'RIGHT-BRAINED' AND THIS HELPS EXPLAIN DIFFERENCES IN HOW WE LEARN."

The other day, I (Yana) gave students in my First Year Experience Seminar a quiz that included true and false statements about learning and the brain. It wasn't for points or anything – I was trying to gauge where the students were, and use the quiz as a jumping-off point for discussion. A lot of students said they believed this statement about the left and right brain. When I asked why they believed this, I received an alarming answer from one student: "My teacher told me."

It is undeniably true that humans have two brain hemispheres. Also, there is scientific evidence (from brain-damaged patients as well as more modern neuroimaging techniques) to suggest that some types of tasks might use more resources from one hemisphere than the other. A good example of this is language, which tends to use more resources from the left hemisphere than the right (Springer & Deutsch, 1998). However, what is NOT true is that individuals can be "right-brained" or "left-brained," or that the former is "creative" while the latter is "rational." This is a misunderstanding of how the brain works: just because some tasks require more resources from one hemisphere, does not mean individuals differ in terms of their brains.

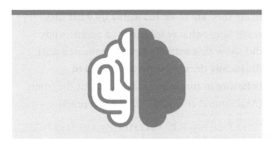

Just because some tasks require more resources from one hemisphere, does not mean individuals differ in terms of their brains.

Even if there were subtle differences between individuals at the level of brain hemispheres, there is no evidence that any of the "left/right brain questionnaires" that pop up frequently on social media would possibly pick up on these differences in any kind of meaningful way. Not to mention the complete lack of relevance of these potential subtle differences to education, contrary to what some for-profit training agencies will claim, e.g., http://kidgeniusapp.com/ – "an application for right brain training," $199/year. Hence, many neuroscientists have come to call this the "left/right brain myth" (Goswami, 2006).

Another important point is that even if some tasks use more resources from one hemisphere than the other, there is no task that exclusively relies on only one hemisphere. As Dr. Melina Uncapher put it,

> *Every complex cognitive function is a result of the engagement of a network of multiple regions, distributed throughout both hemispheres, acting in coordinated ways.* (2016)

Melina Uncapher

Why do people believe this idea? Actually, it's not too different to the issue of learning styles. Since individuals tend to have preferences for certain types of tasks, some find it appealing to label people as "left-brain" or "right-brain" thinkers. For example, if someone likes math, they might be labeled a "left-brain" thinker, whereas if they are good at art they might be classified as a "right-brain" thinker. These categorizations do not serve us well, as they simply push people into boxes and can become self-fulfilling prophesies, preventing the development of novel interests.

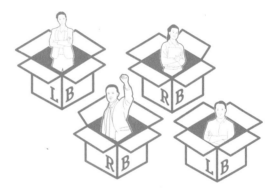

You can read more about this misunderstanding in Melina Uncapher's guest post on our blog (Uncapher, 2016).

MISUNDERSTANDINGS MAY ARISE FROM AN HONEST DESIRE TO LEARN

It is important to emphasize that these misunderstandings do not arise simply because teachers are not paying attention to neuroscience or don't want to learn. In fact, the opposite is true; teachers on the whole find neuroscience useful and important to understand, and find it interesting to explore and learn about (Pickering & Howard-Jones, 2007). However, there is a complex relationship between familiarity with neuroscience and the brain on a basic level, and accurate understanding of the nuances involved.

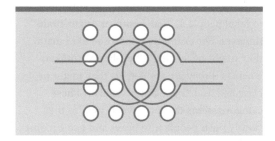

The relationship between interest in neuroscience and accurate understanding of learning is complex.

That is, an active interest in neuroscience unfortunately does not translate into the ability to distinguish between accurate and inaccurate statements about learning and the brain. On the contrary, multiple studies have found small but significant *positive* correlations between accurate general knowledge about the brain and belief in misunderstanding or "neuromyths" (Dekker *et al.*, 2012; Gleichgercht *et al.*, 2015).

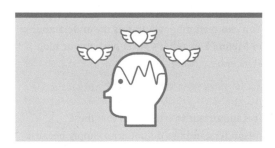

In some cases, those most interested in neuroscience can be more susceptible to believing incorrect information.

That is, to some extent the more a non-expert is curious about neuroscience, the more

likely they are to be led astray by what they read! Somewhat reassuringly, a recent study did show that actually being a neuroscientist drastically decreased the likelihood of believing in misunderstanding about the brain (Macdonald *et al.*, 2017). That's a relief!

WHAT CAN WE DO TO HELP CORRECT THE MISUNDERSTANDINGS?

Let's say you've understood why it is not a good idea to put up too many decorations in a learning environment, but others believe that visual stimulation is important for learning, and don't believe you. Unfortunately, simply providing people with accurate information is often not enough to combat misunderstandings, and can sometimes even create the opposite effect where people dig in to their inaccurate beliefs (Lewandowsky, Ecker, Seifert, Schwarz, & Cook, 2012; Pershan & Riley, 2017).

Shaming people for their beliefs is not an effective way to change minds.

Much research has gone into figuring out the most effective way to correct misunderstandings in an educational setting. One effective technique is called "refutational teaching," and involves the following key stages: facts, refutation, and inoculation (Guzzetti, 2000; Lassonde, Kendeou, & O'Brien, 2016). That is, first of all, you need to start with the correct information (in this case, visually noisy environments lead to distraction and can decrease learning). After that, you would present the misunderstanding – for example, "some people believe that a visually stimulating environment can help children learn, and that this means that classrooms should include lots of bright decorations." Now comes the refutational stage: explain *why* this is not true (see Chapter 9 for more about using "why" questions to increase understanding). Here you would bring in the evidence, referring back to the original factually correct statement. Finally, you can now "inoculate" your audience against the incorrect information, by reminding people of the types of incorrect arguments that tend to come up and how you can refute them. For instance, an argument for visual stimulation in the classroom might be "but children do not learn when they experience sensory deprivation." In the inoculation phase, you would remind your audience that this claim only applies to extreme sensory deprivation, rather than lack of bright pictures in a classroom. You can read more about this method in Annette Taylor's guest post on our blog (Taylor, 2017).

The most important thing is to focus as much as possible on the correct information, rather than repeating the misconception over and over again. That repetition could actually *increase* beliefs of the misunderstanding by causing it to feel more familiar (Lewandowsky *et al.*, 2012; Skurnik, Yoon, Park, & Schwarz, 2005) and making it more memorable in the long run (Peter & Koch, 2016). That's why we have made sure that as you continue to read this book, you will learn about the basic processes of perception, attention, and memory as they are currently understood by cognitive psychological scientists, along with learning strategies that have received decades of evidence to support their effectiveness.

CHAPTER SUMMARY

Unfortunately, misconceptions about ways to improve learning are pervasive in education. For example, it is commonly believed that children in pre-schools need a highly stimulating environment in order to learn best, including many attractive visuals hung on the walls. The research actually shows that while children do need some stimulation, an overload can hinder learning. In this chapter, we discussed why this and other misconceptions have become so pervasive, and why we need to work hard to overcome them, and how we can best do that.

REFERENCES

Dekker, S., Lee, N. C., Howard-Jones, P., & Jolles, J. (2012). Neuromyths in education: Prevalence and predictors of misconceptions among teachers. *Frontiers in Psychology, 3.*

Deligiannidi, K., & Howard-Jones, P. A. (2015). The neuroscience literacy of teachers in Greece. *Procedia-Social and Behavioral Sciences, 174,* 3909–3915.

Diamond, M. C., Krech, D., & Rosenzweig, M. R. (1964). The effects of an enriched environment on the histology of the rat cerebral cortex. *The Journal of Comparative Neurology, 123,* 111–119.

Dündar, S., & Gündüz, N. (2016). Misconceptions regarding the brain: The neuromyths of preservice teachers. *Mind, Brain, and Education, 10,* 212–232.

Erickson, L. (2017, September). Visual "noise", distractibility, and classroom design. *The Learning Scientists Blog.* Retrieved from www.learningscientists.org/blog/2017/9/20-1

Ferrero, M., Garaizar, P., & Vadillo, M. A. (2016). Neuromyths in education: Prevalence among Spanish teachers and an exploration of cross-cultural variation. *Frontiers in Human Neuroscience, 10.*

Fisher, A. V., Godwin, K. E., & Seltman, H. (2014). Visual environment, attention allocation, and learning in young children: When too much of a good thing may be bad. *Psychological Science, 25,* 1362–1370.

Fromkin, V., Krashen, S., Curtiss, S., Rigler, D., & Rigler, M. (1974). The development of language in Genie: A case of language acquisition beyond the "critical period". *Brain and Language, 1,* 81–107.

Gleichgerrcht, E., Luttges, B. L., Salvarezza, F., & Campos, A. L. (2015). Educational neuromyths among teachers in Latin America. *Mind, Brain, and Education, 9,* 170–178.

Goswami, U. (2006). Neuroscience and education: From research to practice? *Nature Reviews Neuroscience, 7,* 406–413.

Guzzetti, B. J. (2000). Learning counter-intuitive science concepts: What have we learned from over a decade of research? *Reading & Writing Quarterly, 16,* 89–98.

Herculano-Houzel, S. (2002). Do you know your brain? A survey on public neuroscience literacy at the closing of the decade of the brain. *The Neuroscientist, 8,* 98–110.

Hermida, M. J., Segretin, M. S., Soni García, A., & Lipina, S. J. (2016). Conceptions and misconceptions about neuroscience in preschool teachers: A study from Argentina. *Educational Research, 58,* 457–472.

Karakus, O., Howard-Jones, P. A., & Jay, T. (2015). Primary and secondary school teachers' knowledge and misconceptions about the brain in Turkey. *Procedia-Social and Behavioral Sciences, 174,* 1933–1940.

Kirschner, P. A. (2017). Stop propagating the learning styles myth. *Computers & Education, 106,* 166–171.

Lassonde, K. A., Kendeou, P., & O'Brien, E. J. (2016). Refutation texts: Overcoming psychology misconceptions that are resistant to change. *Scholarship of Teaching and Learning in Psychology, 2,* 62–74.

Lewandowsky, S., Ecker, U. K., Seifert, C. M., Schwarz, N., & Cook, J. (2012). Misinformation and its correction: Continued influence and successful debiasing. *Psychological Science in the Public Interest, 13,* 106–131.

Macdonald, K., Germine, L., Anderson, A., Christodoulou, J., & McGrath, L. M. (2017). Dispelling the myth: Training in education or neuroscience decreases but does not eliminate beliefs in neuromyths. *Frontiers in Psychology, 8.*

Newton, P. M. (2015). The Learning Styles myth is thriving in higher education. *Frontiers in Psychology, 6.*

Papadatou-Pastou, M., Haliou, E., & Vlachos, F. (2017). Brain knowledge and the prevalence of neuromyths among prospective teachers in Greece. *Frontiers in Psychology, 8.*

Pashler, H., McDaniel, M., Rohrer, D., & Bjork, R. (2009). Learning styles: Concepts and evidence. *Psychological Science in the Public Interest, 9,* 105–119.

Pei, X., Howard-Jones, P. A., Zhang, S., Liu, X., & Jin, Y. (2015). Teachers' understanding about the brain in East China. *Procedia-Social and Behavioral Sciences, 174,* 3681–3688.

Pershan, M., & Riley, B. (2017, October). Why mythbusting fails: A guide to influencing education with science [Blog post]. *Deans for Impact.* Retrieved from https://deansforimpact.org/why-mythbusting-fails-a-guide-to-influencing-education-with-science/

Peter, C., & Koch, T. (2016). When debunking scientific myths fails (and when it does not): The backfire effect in the context of journalistic coverage and immediate judgments as prevention strategy. *Science Communication, 38,* 3–25.

Pickering, S. J., & Howard-Jones, P. (2007). Educators' views on the role of neuroscience in education: Findings from a study of UK and international perspectives. *Mind, Brain, and Education, 1,* 109–113.

Skurnik, I., Yoon, C., Park, D., & Schwarz, N. (2005). How warnings about false claims become recommendations. *Journal of Consumer Research, 31,* 713–724.

Springer, S. P., & Deutsch, G. (1998). *A series of books in psychology. Left brain, right brain: Perspectives from cognitive neuroscience,* 5th ed. New York: W. H. Freeman/Times Books/ Henry Holt & Co.

Taylor, A. (2017). How to help students overcome misconceptions [Blog post]. *The Learning Scientists Blog.* Retrieved from www.learningscientists.org/blog/2017/7/25-1

Vernon, J. A., & Hoffman, J. (1956). Effect of sensory deprivation upon rote learning in human beings. *Science, 123,* 1074–1075.

Uncapher, M. (2016, August). Exploring the left brain/right brain myth [Blog post]. *The Learning Scientists Blog.* Retrieved from www.learningscientists.org/blog/2016/8/2-1

Part 2

BASICS OF HUMAN COGNITIVE PROCESSES

Perception allows us to make sense of the world.

Sensation is objective, whereas perception is subjective.

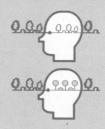

What one perceives differs from person to person, and from situation to situation.

Bottom-up processing begins and ends with the stimulus.

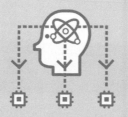

Top-down processing involves applying prior knowledge to understanding a situation.

Humans tend to mostly engage in a lot of top-down processing.

Students bring different types and levels of knowledge to the classroom.

As teachers, we need to be sensitive to different levels of understanding.

The curse of knowledge means that teachers can sometimes lack awareness of how students process information.

PERCEPTION

Information is interpreted differently depending on the context and the person – there are no absolutes. As teachers, we need to be sensitive to these differences, which sometimes means taking another's perspectives.

Before we can talk about learning, we have to talk about perception. This is because perception determines how we understand the world.

Perception allows us to make sense of the world.

Although we will focus on vision and hearing in this chapter, because they are arguably most relevant to learning in an academic context, we should emphasize that perception involves all five of our senses: vision, hearing, touch, taste, and smell. Let's start with an example from hearing. Imagine you are alone, hiking in a forest. All of a sudden, you hear a loud cracking noise. How do you react? Do you think it's a branch and keep walking? Do you think it's a gunshot and get scared? Do you think it's a gun shot and *not* get scared, because you know that there are hunters

nearby and you've taken the right precautions to avoid the designated hunting area? If you thought it was a branch, you probably didn't have much of a reaction. But if you thought it was a gunshot, your heart rate might have risen, more or less depending on your familiarity with the layout of the forest (Goldstein, 2009).

This example illustrates that the way we interpret something (in this case, a sound) depends on what we know about it. But knowing that the crack is a cracking branch rather than a gunshot doesn't literally change the sound waves – it only changes the way you hear them. This is the key to the difference between sensation and perception. Sensation is the signals received by your organs through the five senses, whereas perception is the *interpretation* of those signals. Sensation is objective, whereas perception is subjective.

Sensation is objective, whereas perception is subjective.

That is, what one perceives differs from person to person, and from situation to situation. A very simple visual example of this is that the same square of color will look different under different circumstances.

This picture shows two small rectangles surrounded by larger rectangles. Look at the two small rectangles. Are they the same color? It looks like the one on the left is lighter and the one on the right is darker – right? Actually, they are the same. The reason why the one on the left looks lighter is that it is surrounded by a darker square.

Here is the same picture, but now we have removed the larger surrounding rectangles. In this picture, you can clearly see that the two small rectangles are the same color. For some of us, it is really hard to believe that the two small boxes in the first image are actually the same color. The illusion is very powerful, demonstrating the importance of context in perception. The sensations we are receiving from the small rectangles are unchanged, but our perception of their color is affected by other colors around them.

These pictures show two people standing at different distances from the camera. The person standing closest to the camera holds out their hand, and places it "under" the feet of the person standing further away, making it look as though they are holding a tiny person in the palm of their hand. In this illusion, the juxtaposition of the two people leads to a temporary suspension of the size constancy principle (Boring, 1940). Somewhat counterintuitively, what we are perceiving in these pictures is a more accurate representation of our visual input! The size constancy principle is an example of the difference between sensation and perception because even though the sensations sent through our eyes to our brain show objects changing size as they move closer or further away from us, we're able to adjust our perception to understand that the object is just moving rather than changing size.

In the next column you'll see another example from vision: when things move towards you, they look like they're getting bigger, and when things move away from you, they look like they're getting smaller; but in reality, they are staying the same size, and that's how we see it (this effect is known as the size constancy principle; Boring, 1940). Our brains find a way of compensating for this – but only if we have the relevant context cues.

PERCEPTION IN EDUCATION

But, this type of context-dependent, subjective perception shows up in more academically relevant settings as well. We may think that we are giving our students knowledge and assessing it in a neutral and impartial way, but students will bring to the table their own preconceived notions, reactions, and attitudes to the material. Similarly, students bring their own perspective to teaching strategies and assessment techniques. For example, Sambell and McDowell (1998) conducted in-depth interviews with university students in the

UK to examine their attitudes towards various types of assessment, including closed-book versus open-book exams. While one student said that the two types of exams seemed very different and would require different preparation techniques, another student expressed that she would study in exactly the same way for an open-book exam as for a closed-book exam, because in her mind both were testing the same thing.

Newborn babies engage mostly in bottom-up processing: their attention is caught by bright, shiny, and loud things in their environment. If they hear a fire alarm, they may show discomfort, be startled, or cry; but they are not thinking about what the alarm means ("Oh no, it might be a fire!" or "There goes the drill we were warned about").

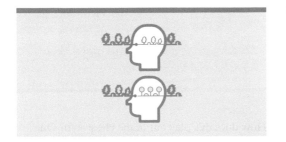

What one perceives differs from person to person, and from situation to situation.

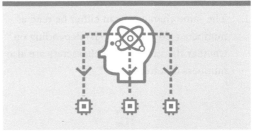

Top-down processing involves applying prior knowledge to understanding a situation.

When we talk about perception, we usually distinguish between bottom-up and top-down processing of information. This distinction is important to understand. Bottom-up processing begins and ends with the stimulus. You focus on the information coming from whatever you are trying to perceive, and you try to understand it without bringing your prior knowledge to bear on the situation.

Top-down processing, on the other hand, involves bringing your prior knowledge to bear on your interpretation of the input you are receiving. In the case of the fire alarm above, an adult would bring their knowledge of the source of the noise (recognizing that it is an alarm) and any other information they might have (e.g., having been warned about a drill), and act accordingly (scared, surprised, or just annoyed).

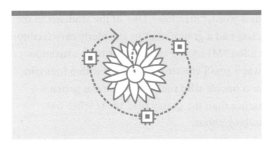

Bottom-up processing begins and ends with the stimulus.

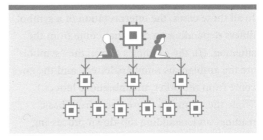

Humans tend to mostly engage in a lot of top-down processing.

We tend to think that when we look at something, we are piecing together what is really there (bottom-up processing). Of course, we are always using bottom-up processing as different stimuli hit our senses. However, as you will see, humans use top-down processing much more than we might realize.

The act of reading provides us with many examples of this:

1. The same characters can either be read as numbers (13) or a letter (B) depending on whether the surrounding characters are also numbers or letters:

2. The same character can be read either as an H or as an A, depending on what letters surrounded it:

3. We automatically complete words by inferring the appropriate hidden letter.

L**ARNING

In all these cases, the interpretation of a symbol differs depending on cues that come from the situation. (In the examples above, the "symbols" are the ambiguous numbers/letters, and the cues come from the other, unambiguous letters.) While the examples above come from basic reading, understanding top-down processing helps us realize the importance of learners' perspectives and background knowledge. Students bring different experiences as well as different types and levels of knowledge to

the classroom, and these will affect how they perceive information presented to them in class.

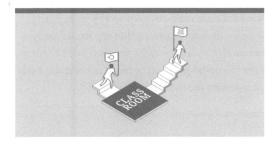

Students bring different types and levels of knowledge to the classroom.

How does this play out in the classroom? One student might be able to link an abstract idea back to a concrete example from their own life, making it more salient and easier to remember later (Schuh, 2016); while another student who has not had an experience related to this idea may only interpret the concept abstractly, making it more difficult to remember later (see Chapter 9 for more on how concrete information is remembered more easily than abstract information). Or, a student may interpret a concept using a concrete example from their life that is not exactly what the teacher had in mind. In the book *Making Meaning by Making Connections*, Schuh (2016, p. 5) describes how a teacher was trying to get students to learn a new word, "meadow." One of the students in the class had a grandfather in an elderly care facility called "Meadow Farm," so for him, a meadow was a small cluster of buildings with a fountain and people who took care of stroke patients – rather than the grassy field the teacher was talking about.

It is also possible that some students might have an emotional reaction to something presented in class, making them more prone to thinking about something other than what they are trying to learn (Mrazek *et al.*, 2011; see Chapter 6 for more information about this thought process, which we call "mind-wandering") while others remain unaffected and stay tuned into the material being presented. Students from different cultures may also have different reactions to instructional techniques, and different motivations for learning (Shechter, Durik, Miyamoto, & Harackiewicz, 2011). And, the types of questions students ask about material will depend on their prior knowledge (Miyake & Norman, 1979). Realizing that these differences exist, right from the beginning when students are first encountering material in a class, is an important step towards making knowledge accessible to all students.

As teachers, we need to be sensitive to different levels of understanding.

In an educational context, we might think about "rote memorization" (remembering information without necessarily understanding it) as relying mostly on bottom-up processing, whereas understanding a concept and being able to describe it in your own words relies more on top-down processing. Although the latter is what we strive for, some have argued that both memorization and development of understanding are equally important to learning (Kember, 1996).

THE CURSE OF KNOWLEDGE

The curse of knowledge is the phenomenon of thinking something is easy or obvious because you

have had a lot of experience with it (Nickerson, 1999). In our case, we are extremely familiar with terms related to memory. When describing a concept such as retrieval practice to a student, we might accidentally use other terms that are unfamiliar to the student. For example, we might talk about bringing information that has already been encoded to mind from memory. If the student is unfamiliar with the concept of "encoding," they might be confused by our definition. Or, we might tell the student to practice free recall or cued recall during studying, and then later realize we need to explain what recall is, as well as the difference between free recall and cued recall. (In case you are wondering, free recall involves writing down everything you know from memory without using any cues, whereas cued recall could be something like answering specific questions about the information.)

The curse of knowledge means that sometimes we as teachers can lack awareness of how students process information. Though we, of course, were also once students who did not know anything about the subject we are teaching, it is hard for us to "unlearn" the information and put ourselves in a student's shoes to experience the novelty of learning about this concept.

The curse of knowledge means that teachers can sometimes lack awareness of how students process information.

When writing this book, we had to be very careful to check our writing and make sure we weren't including terms and concepts without defining them – this is why we've included a glossary along with this book! For example, in Chapter 10 we try our best to bypass the curse of knowledge and explain how retrieval practice can be used in the classroom and at home.

What can be done about the curse of knowledge? Nickerson (1999) recommends that you can deliberately mitigate your own overconfidence by thinking about possible alternative answers or explanations (Arkes, Christensen, Lai & Blumer, 1987). For example, a student or even a friend might say something that you think is wrong, but on further consideration you may realize that they were just presenting an alternative explanation that is equally valid. Also, when trying to explain something that you know well, you can try to paraphrase it. You may find that explaining it in your own words is more difficult than you expected, and this feeling of difficulty will be more closely related to a student's experience with the material than your own fluency in processing the familiar formulation (Kelley, 1999). The most important thing is to realize that the way you happen to think about any concept is not absolute – others may be coming from a different place and will engage with it in a different way (Jacoby, Bjork, & Kelley, 1994).

CHAPTER SUMMARY

The difference between sensation and perception serves to explain why we don't always experience the world exactly how it is, or in the same way as the next person. When we talk about perception, we usually distinguish between bottom-up and top-down processing of information. Bottom-up processing begins and ends with the stimulus: you focus on the information coming from whatever you are trying to perceive, and you try to understand it just by using this information. Though we are always using bottom-up processing, we are usually also engaged in top-down processing, whereby we use our

knowledge to understand something. This top-down processing can result in different interpretations of the information and strategies we try to teach our students, as well as a "curse of knowledge" that makes it difficult for us to see things through a novice's eyes.

REFERENCES

Arkes, H. R., Christensen, C., Lai, C., & Blumer, C. (1987). Two methods of reducing overconfidence. *Organizational Behavior and Human Decision Processes, 39,* 133–144.

Boring, E. G. (1940). Size constancy and Emmert's law. *The American Journal of Psychology, 53,* 293–295.

Goldstein, B. E. (2009). *Sensation and Perception,* 8th (Ed.) Belmont, CA: Cengage Learning.

Jacoby, L. L., Bjork, R. A., & Kelley, C. M. (1994). Illusions of comprehension, competence, and remembering. In D. Druckman & R. A. Bjork (Eds.), *Learning, remembering, believing: Enhancing human performance* (pp. 57–80). Washington, DC: National Academy Press

Kelley, C. M. (1999). Subjective experience as a basis of "objective" judgments: Effects of past experience on judgments of difficulty. In D. Gopher & A. Koriat (Eds.), *Attention and performance XVII: Cognitive regulation of performance: Interaction of theory and application* (pp. 515–536). Cambridge, MA: MIT Press.

Kember, D. (1996). The intention to both memorise and understand: Another approach to learning? *Higher Education, 31,* 341–354.

Miyake, N., & Norman, D. A. (1979). To ask a question, one must know enough to know what is not known. *Journal of Verbal Learning and Verbal Behavior, 18,* 357–364.

Mrazek, M. D., Chin, J. M., Schmader, T., Hartson, K. A., Smallwood, J., & Schooler, J. W. (2011). Threatened to distraction: Mind-wandering as a consequence of stereotype threat. *Journal of Experimental Social Psychology, 47,* 1243–1248.

Nickerson, R. S. (1999). How we know—and sometimes misjudge—what others know: Imputing one's own knowledge to others. *Psychological Bulletin, 125,* 737–759.

Sambell, K., & McDowell, L. (1998). The construction of the hidden curriculum: Messages and meanings in the assessment of student learning. *Assessment & Evaluation in Higher Education, 23,* 391–402.

Schuh, K. L. (2016). *Making Meaning by Making Connections.* Dordrecht, Netherlands: Springer.

Shechter, O. G., Durik, A. M., Miyamoto, Y., & Harackiewicz, J. M. (2011). The role of utility value in achievement behavior: The importance of culture. *Personality and Social Psychology Bulletin, 37,* 303–317.

Attention is a cognitive process that is very hard to pin down.

Attention is typically thought of as a "limited-capacity resource."

Cognitive Load Theory has helped teachers focus on the efficiency of their explanations to avoid any inadvertent overload.

An important feature of attention is the ability to selectively focus on just one stimulus at a time.

Switching between two tasks decreases efficiency and slows down reaction speeds in both tasks.

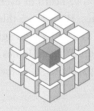

The likelihood that a student will pay attention is determined in part by the saliency of the material.

Both individual and situational interest affect the extent to which we pay attention in a learning situation.

Mind-wandering involves getting distracted from a task by your own thoughts.

Mind-wandering can be problematic because it can result in students missing important information.

ATTENTION

Attention is notoriously hard to define, but is essential for learning to occur. Our attentional resources are limited and must be directed towards the most important information.

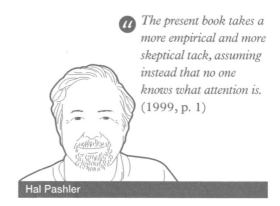

Hal Pashler

The present book takes a more empirical and more skeptical tack, assuming instead that no one knows what attention is. (1999, p. 1)

"Pay attention!" "You're not paying attention." "If only you had been paying attention…"

Surely, you've heard or even said such things many times. But what *is* this attention that we speak of? Do we have an agreed-upon definition of attention? William James (often known as the father of psychology) seemed to think that we do:

Everyone knows what attention is. It is the taking possession by the mind, in clear and vivid form, of one out of what seem several simultaneously possible objects or trains of thought. (1890, pp. 403–404)

William James

In fact, many researchers are indeed unsure about the nature of attention – though they have tried to capture and define this elusive concept. Is attention a physical thing? What does it mean to "pay" attention – is it like a fee? What does it mean to "give something your full attention"? Is attention a cause (e.g., something that helps learning), or an effect (e.g., something that is increased by learning; Anderson, 2011)?

Attention is a cognitive process that is very hard to pin down.

In the introduction to his book on attention published more than a century later, on the other hand, cognitive psychologist Hal Pashler took the opposite stance:

It turns out that attention is very hard to pin down – so hard that certain contemporary researchers have thrown up their hands and decided that perhaps attention as it is currently

defined cannot be studied: Britt Anderson discussed this in his provocatively titled article, "There is no Such Thing as Attention":

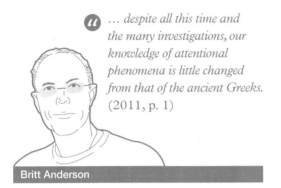

> *... despite all this time and the many investigations, our knowledge of attentional phenomena is little changed from that of the ancient Greeks.* (2011, p. 1)

Britt Anderson

Attention is typically thought of as a "limited-capacity resource."

Nevertheless, most cognitive psychologists do agree that attention is an important concept to teach their students. The most commonly accepted definition of attention among cognitive psychologists is focus on a specific stimulus, or the ability to focus on specific stimuli or locations (if talking about an individual difference).

The same can be said of attention, according to the limited capacity resource model: you have a certain amount of attention, and you apportion it to different tasks. If you're doing a really difficult task that requires a lot of attention to be paid to it, you won't have much attention left for anything else. If you're doing an easy task, you might have some attention "left over" for other tasks.

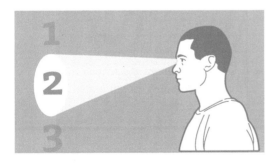

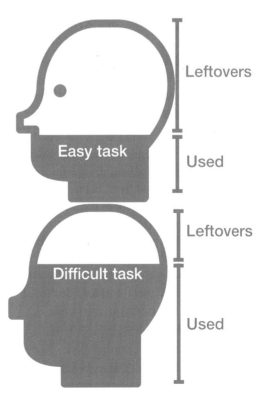

Attention is typically thought of as a "limited-capacity resource" (Moray, 1967). You might think of your financial budget as an analogy. You have a certain amount of money, and you apportion it to different expenses. If you spend a lot of money on a dress this month, you might not be able to eat out. If you had bought the cheap dress instead, you may have been able to afford a meal at a fancy restaurant.

COGNITIVE LOAD

Cognitive Load Theory has helped teachers focus on the efficiency of their explanations to avoid any inadvertent overload.

The idea that we have limited attentional resources places a certain limitation on how much information we can process at any one time. The amount of information requiring our attention is known in the literature as "cognitive load," and an overabundance of it is known as "cognitive overload" (Sweller & Chandler, 1994). Two theories of cognitive load have dominated the field: one known simply as Load Theory (Lavie, Hirst, De Fockert, & Viding, 2004), and the other as Cognitive Load Theory (CLT; Chandler & Sweller, 1991).

Lavie's Load Theory distinguishes between different types of load: perceptual load, which describes the amount of bottom-up information that has to be processed (see Chapter 5), and cognitive load, which describes the demand on working memory (see below). This theory is rather nuanced, and allows us to disentangle positive and negative impacts of load on learning. For example, a recent study showed that while increased perceptual load decreased memory for an advertisement, increased cognitive load actually increased learning (Wang & Duff, 2016).

Sweller's Cognitive Load Theory is more familiar to teachers, as much of the work on this theory has been applied directly to education (e.g., Chandler & Sweller, 1991; Chang & Ley, 2006). The basic idea behind this theory is that since we can only process a limited amount of information at any one time, it is very important to avoid overloading attention with unnecessary or extraneous material. This has implications for how we design presentations, write textbooks, and create multimedia materials (Mayer & Moreno, 2003). In Chapters 9 and 11, we talk more about how to reduce cognitive overload.

THE MYTH OF MULTI-TASKING

You probably don't realize this, but an important feature of your attentional mechanism – no matter which of the theories above you subscribe to – is being able to selectively focus on just *one* stimulus (a location, object, or message) at any one time.

An important feature of attention is the ability to selectively focus on just one stimulus at a time.

We are now going to tell you something you will have trouble believing. The data point strongly to the conclusion that it is *almost impossible* to pay attention to more than one thing at the exact same time. You might protest – "but I can drive while listening to music, I can eat while reading a book, I can have the TV on in the background while studying these lecture notes." I wonder how many of you have some kind of distraction – be it the TV, music, kids, or a partner – present while you are reading this sentence? You may not think that the thing you listed is a distraction at all. Perhaps it's something you are used to having on in the background (e.g., the TV), or something that you feel is complementary rather than interfering with this material (e.g., music).

Well, it turns out that your intuitions are almost certainly wrong. If you are paying attention to this sentence, you're probably not meaningfully processing the music. If you are able to tell me in detail what is happening on the TV, you probably couldn't give me a good summary of what you've just read – at least, not as good as if you were fully focusing on the one task. But if you still feel like you can do these things, then you may have figured out how to switch back and forth between the two tasks very quickly. When you feel like you're multi-tasking, or paying attention to two things at once, you're actually switching back and forth between the two things you're trying to pay attention to, and as we'll learn later, that diminishes efficiency for both of the tasks.

One important aspect of attention is the finding that going back and forth between two different tasks involves switch costs that decrease efficiency and slow down reaction speeds *in both tasks* (Gopher, Armony, & Greenshpan, 2000).

Here is a very simple yet powerful demonstration of task switching costs that you can try out on your own or – if you are a teacher – with a class

Switching between two tasks decreases efficiency and slows down reaction speeds in both tasks.

of students. This is a demonstration that students can take part in alone, in pairs, in groups of three, or as a class with one student volunteering to be the "case study" that the rest of the class observes. In this demonstration, students are invited to time themselves performing two separate tasks, and then attempting to switch back and forth between the two tasks.

THE DEMONSTRATION

The demonstration involves doing three very short tasks:

- Task 1 is counting up from 1 to 26.
- Task 2 is reciting the alphabet from A to Z.
- Task 3 is interleaving numbers with letters, 1-A-2-B-3-C etc. – that is, switching back and forth between Tasks 1 and 2.

Yep, that's it! If you want to do this task on yourself, you can simply do each of the three tasks, and time yourself completing each one. Try it right now – before you read the rest of the chapter.

How long did each of the three tasks take you to complete? I (Yana) had 27 students in my online class complete the three tasks alone and tell me the time it took them to complete each task (in seconds) as part of a weekly quiz. Here were the results:

- Task 1 (counting from 1 to 26) took 5–48 seconds
- Task 2 (reciting the alphabet) took 3–22 seconds
- Task 3 (switching back and forth) took 27–110 seconds.

Importantly, every single student took longer to complete the combined Task 3 than the sum of the time it took them to complete both of the other tasks (Task 1 + Task 2). So, every student in my sample experienced task-switching costs.

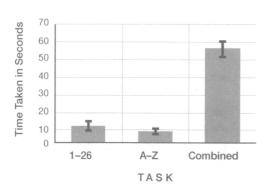

If you want to use the demonstration as a classroom activity, you can try it out in various ways. In pairs, one student can act as the timer and the other as the participant (this will take about five minutes). Also in pairs, students can take turns to act as timer and participant (this will take about ten minutes, and is good for smaller groups if you want to generate sufficient data to analyze as a class). An alternative version that does not require students breaking out into groups is to ask one volunteer to demonstrate all three tasks in front of the class. Since

task-switching costs in this paradigm are so robust, even a single-participant case study can serve to demonstrate the effect.

WHAT DRIVES ATTENTION TOWARDS LEARNING?

The Increased Saliency Theory of attention states that attentional resources constantly shift around so that some things become more salient than others – that is, more noticeable or important. For instance, let's say you're looking at a Where's Waldo? puzzle or Where's Wally? puzzle (US and UK terminology for the game, respectively). Everyone is wearing the same kind of outfit as him, so it's nearly impossible to find him. Your job is to direct your attention to Waldo, but your attention is being directed all over the picture because everyone looks like Waldo! Now imagine I remove the color from the image, except for the area in which you can find Waldo, so that everything except Waldo is in black and white. Bam! Now Waldo pops out.

The Increased Salience Theory describes attention in terms of this kind of pop-out effect – whatever it is we are currently paying attention to is highlighted in our minds. For instance, let's say I ask you to count all of the things in your current location that are colored red. Isn't it amazing that you can glance around and pick out those things, ignoring everything else? That is attentional focus due to increased salience.

In an educational context, the degree to which students are paying attention to what they are trying to learn can be determined to some extent by the saliency of the material.

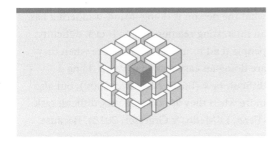

The likelihood that a student will pay attention is determined in part by the saliency of the material.

This saliency can come from many sources: it can be coming from the student's own motivation, the interest level of the material in terms of meaning, the way the information is presented by the teacher, or even more bottom-up features such as bright colors and loud sounds (see Chapter 5 for more on bottom-up and top-down processes).

Yana occasionally claps her hands or says a loud unexpected word in the middle of class to draw students' attention back to the lesson! Megan sometimes says to her students, if she thinks they're not fully attending to the lesson: raise your hand if you're breathing. And then becomes silent. Some students chuckle and raise their hands. Some, who were only partially paying attention to the lesson, look around the room, a bit confused, while raising their hands. Finally, the remainder of students all of a sudden get the sense that a question was asked and realize they have shifted their attention to something else entirely!

Hidi and Harackiewicz (2000) distinguished between two types of interest that an individual can have in a subject: individual interest, and situational interest. Using this book as an example, individual interest is the extent to which you yourself are already interested in applying cognitive psychology to education, whereas situational interest is how absorbing our text is or how enjoyable you find the illustrations. In an educational setting, for example, a high school student may have a personal interest in gender, so they pay more attention in classes that are relevant to this topic than any other classes. Or, students might have a goal that is addressed by certain classes more than others – for example, they may be interested in a chemistry class if they plan to go on to medical school.

Situational interest, on the other hand, is how engaging the teacher makes the class. Situational interest can be increased through many different teaching techniques: for example, through clear communication of ideas targeted at the right difficulty level (Rotgans & Schmidt, 2011), social activities such as having students research information and then teach each other (Hidi, Weiss, Berndorff, & Nolan, 1998), and using concrete examples (Tapola, Veermans, & Niemivirta, 2013; see also Chapter 9). Both individual and situational interest affect the extent to which we pay attention in a learning situation. As teachers, we are in control of situational interest, but not of individual interest.

Both individual and situational interest affect the extent to which we pay attention in a learning situation.

Note that this is not the same thing as intrinsic versus extrinsic motivation, which, broadly speaking, describes whether students are driven by learning for its own sake, or external rewards and punishments (Reiss, 2012). This distinction is particularly important because extrinsic rewards and punishments can be detrimental to existing intrinsic motivation (Deci, Koestner, & Ryan, 1999; though, note that when there is a lack of intrinsic motivation, such as in dull tasks, extrinsic motivation can be helpful [Deci, Koestner, & Ryan, 2001]). On the other hand, situational interest has not been found to undermine inherent interest – on the contrary, situational interest can actually help maintain or even strengthen inherent interest (Hidi & Harackiewicz, 2000).

WHAT ARE THE CONSEQUENCES OF NOT PAYING ATTENTION?

No matter how motivated you are, you must admit that sometimes you get distracted from what you are supposed to be doing or thinking about. When these distractions come from inside your head, psychologists call them mind-wandering (Smallwood & Schooler, 2006). Cognitive psychologists refer to things you are intending to be paying attention to as a "task set." For instance, if your intention is to be reading this chapter, then your current task set is "reading the chapter." If you start having

unrelated or irrelevant thoughts while reading these words, such as "I wonder what I'll be eating for dinner," this would be classified as losing the task set of "reading the chapter."

Mind-wandering levels vary depending on what the person is doing. Mind-wandering has an interesting relationship with task difficulty: people tend to mind-wander more when they are doing an easy task than when doing a difficult task (Forster & Lavie, 2009), but also more when they are doing a very difficult task (Feng, D'Mello, & Graesser, 2013). Because of these differences, as well as differences in methodologies for measuring mind-wandering (Weinstein, 2018), it is difficult and perhaps almost meaningless to give an "average" mind-wandering rate. However, researchers have proposed that about half the time, students are not paying attention to what the teacher is saying in class (Smallwood, Fishman, & Schooler, 2007).

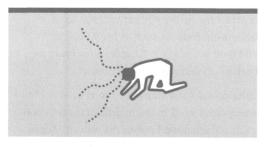

Mind-wandering can be problematic because it can result in students missing important information.

Early in the 20th century, researchers tried to measure mind-wandering in the classroom. In 1941, Edmiston and Braddock had observers record whether students were attending to a lecture by identifying any behavior such as a "physical attitude" or "expression of the eyes" that suggested students were no longer attending to the lesson.

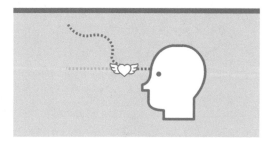

Mind-wandering involves getting distracted from a task by your own thoughts.

A student in Cohen *et al.*'s (1956) bell-pushing study

In 1956, Cohen, Hansel, and Sylvester put students in a classroom with bell-pushes every desk, and students were asked to push the bell to indicate that their minds had wandered away from the lecture; the information fed through to a light in an adjacent room, and the average number of mind-wandering reports were presented in the paper in five-minute increments. Cohen *et al.* reported that mind-wandering varied widely from student to student.

Most mind-wandering research has used adults as participants. However, children are thought to develop the ability to engage in self-regulated learning by the age of 11 (Roebers, 2006). Mrazek, Phillips, Franklin, Broadway, and Schooler (2013) gathered mind-wandering data from middle and high school students. This study demonstrated that students as young as those in 6th grade are able to accurately report on the focus of their thoughts. In addition, mind-wandering was also negatively related to comprehension in this young sample.

When we are trying to understand and learn, we need to combine whatever we are studying with our internal world. Mind-wandering can be problematic when it comes to education because it can result in students missing important information (Smallwood *et al.*, 2007). The amount of mind-wandering students report during study

correlates with later reading comprehension (Smallwood, McSpadden, & Schooler, 2008) and memory performance (Risko, Anderson, Sarwal, Engelhardt, & Kingstone, 2012), though it is important to note that this correlation does not mean that mind-wandering *causes* poor performance (see Chapter 2).

Finally, mind-wandering can occur not only during study, but also during a test. Students themselves believe that mind-wandering during a test leads to poor time management and possible exam failure (Ling, Heffernan, & Muncer, 2003).

CAPACITY OF SHORT-TERM MEMORY

One area of intense research has focused around the capacity of short-term memory, not just in terms of time, but in terms of how many separate pieces of information can be stored in short-term memory for any one time. The simplest task used to measure the capacity of short-term memory is the "memory span task." In the experiment, the experimenter will read out a series of digits to the participant, and the participant will try to repeat them back in the same order. If they succeed, the number of digits is increased for the next trial, until they are no longer able to correctly repeat back the numbers in order. So, if you correctly repeated back eight digits but failed when there were nine, you would be said to have a "digit span" of eight. Most people tend to have a digit span of five to nine items.

Only five to nine items? That seems like very little. However, our clever minds come to the rescue, as we have actually found a way to circumvent this limitation. Here's how. Imagine we asked you to repeat back from memory the following string of letter and numbers, in this order:

E T 6 N A H C O T E P R I T A T N

It should be fairly obvious that if you tried to repeat this back without looking at the page, you wouldn't get the whole string correct (but do try it for yourself!).

What if we rearranged these letter and numbers into something more meaningful?

CHAPTER 6 ATTENTION

All of a sudden, it's a piece of cake! That's because of something we call "chunking" (yes, that's a real, scientific term). Chunking allows for more information to be stored in short-term memory, so that you're still only remembering five to nine items, but each item contains more information. One subject, S. F., was able to increase his digit span to roughly 80 digits (Ericsson & Chase, 1982)! That's right, the researcher read off 80 digits, and the subject was able to recite them back in the same order. This took hundreds of hours of practice across two years, and the subject had to chunk the numbers into meaningful units for himself (track times with which he was familiar). Of course, we don't really need to increase our short-term memory capacities in this way, and increasing our digit span isn't likely to help us learn and remember educationally relevant material.

However, while researchers originally thought of short-term memory as just a very small temporary storage capacity, after this initial approach cognitive psychologists realized that short-term memory actually did a lot more than simply store information. In addition to storage, our short-term memory processes also allow us to manipulate information (e.g., doing mathematical calculations in your head) and switch between tasks – though not as efficiently as if you were just doing one task at a time.

However, in the context of learning information in the long run, what's most important is getting that information from short-term into long-term memory. Your short-term memory process essentially decides what's worth keeping and what can be forgotten after the 15–30-second window (see Chapter 7).

WORKING MEMORY

Cognitive psychologists have attempted to describe the processes involved in attention through a model called "working memory." What do we mean by a model? A cognitive model can be thought of as a framework that defines various different processes that go on in the mind. In this particular case, it is a model that describes our ability to hold information for a short time, manipulate it, send it to/from long-term memory, and it can help us switch between tasks (though not particularly efficiently, as you read above). In particular, cognitive psychologists are interested in three key processes that they believe define working memory: the phonological loop, the visuospatial sketchpad, and the central executive (Baddeley & Hitch, 1974; Baddeley, 2003).

The phonological loop stores and also rehearses verbal/auditory information. "Rehearsal" is essentially just repeating things over and over in your head so that you can remember it for a little while. It's a way of getting around the short time span of short-term memory, and you probably do this without realizing. Imagine you are on your smartphone looking up a phone number. But annoyingly, when you get to the number you can't just tap it to make the call because it's not in the right format (it's not a clickable link). Instead, you have to remember the number while you switch from your browser app to your phone app and then type in the number. In order to hold the number in your mind, you start reciting it subvocally (in your head), "555 6792, 555 6792, 555 6792" until you're finally able to type it in. When you're reciting in this example, you're using your phonological loop.

If your phonological loop is busy doing something else, though, it won't help you retain information. What if I asked you to remember that phone number while repeating "the-the-the" out loud? What would happen is that you would have a harder time remembering the number, because your phonological loop was busy with the noise of "the-the-the" and so could not effectively rehearse the numbers you were trying to remember.

The visuospatial sketchpad, on the other hand, helps you store visual information and plan using visual imagery. The visuospatial sketchpad enables you to create mental maps and spatial images. For example, imagine I asked you how you get from your bedroom to your kitchen. You might answer this question by picturing yourself walking through your house from one room to the other. This imagination process is thought to utilize the visuospatial sketchpad.

The visuospatial sketchpad appears to work somewhat independently from the phonological loop. For example, if I was asking you to do a visual imagery task instead of remembering a phone number as in the previous example, you might be able to repeat the sound "the-the-the" and still do the visual imagery task; this suggests that the visuospatial sketchpad and phonological loop involve separate cognitive processes.

The third and final process of the working memory model is called the central executive. It is still not completely clear what this part of the model does, but it is generally thought to involve all of the remaining processes of working memory, and is very closely linked to attention: determining what specifically to focus on, determining what information to send to/from long-term memory, and interfacing between the phonological loop and visuospatial sketchpad.

INDIVIDUAL DIFFERENCES IN ATTENTION

Many theories have tried to account for individual differences in attention and its components. One of the difficulties involved in making sense of these theories is that the terminology has evolved over the years. For example, the notion of mind-wandering has been mentioned in the educational literature

since as early as the 19th century (Loisette, 1896). Researchers have called it different things throughout the years: goal neglect (Kane & Engle, 2003); stimulus-independent thought (Teasdale *et al.*, 1995); day-dreaming (Schupak & Rosenthal, 2009); and absent-mindedness (Reason & Mycielska, 1982).

Regardless of the label used, the tendency to disengage from concentrating on a task differs from person to person and throughout the life span. For example, older adults tend to report less mind-wandering than younger adults (Jackson & Balota, 2012). Other things that may be related to mind-wandering are individual differences in distractibility (Forster & Lavie, 2014) and mood (negative mind-wandering leading to greater mind-wandering; Smallwood, Fitzgerald, Miles, & Phillips, 2009).

Mind-wandering also has a complex and heavily disputed relationship with individual differences in attention (McVay & Kane, 2012). Below we describe three theories that have attempted to account for individual differences in attention, and why some people might find it more difficult than others to direct and maintain focus.

Theory 1 of 3: Working memory capacity
As we described above, working memory allows you to juggle things in your head (such as if I ask you to multiply 15 by 7), and it allows you to remember the beginning of this sentence without glancing back up a few lines. The *Working Memory Theory* of attention states that the amount of "attentional resources" we have is dependent on how much information we can hold and manipulate at any one time. This theory is popular in educational contexts, as some studies have shown correlations between working memory capacity and academic performance (e.g., Gathercole, Pickering, Knight, & Stegmann, 2004).

Theory 2 of 3: Processing speed

The Processing Speed Theory involves describing our attentional resources in terms of how quickly we can process information (Kail & Salthouse, 1994). The idea is that we learn how to do very simple tasks very fast. These simple tasks could be something like recognizing shapes, colors, and letters. According to this theory, our attentional resources capacity is dependent upon how quickly we can do these simple tasks – the quicker we can process things, the better we can perform on tasks that require us to process multiple pieces of information. This is another theory that has been linked to education, with correlations between processing speed and academic achievement (e.g., Bull & Johnston, 1997).

Theory 3 of 3: Attentional control

The Attentional Control Theory, on the other hand, puts the onus on our ability to focus on whatever we choose in any given moment. According to this theory, those who have better attentional control are able to more effectively select what to focus on, and maintain this focus for longer without getting distracted or starting to mind-wander (McVay & Kane, 2009). Having said that, attentional control alone cannot account for all of the variation between individuals in terms of mind-wandering, suggesting that other factors are also at play (Stawarczyk, Majerus, Catale, & D'Argembeau, 2014).

It is far beyond the scope of this book for us to distinguish between these theories; in fact, no scientific consensus has yet been reached, so this would not even be possible. The big picture is that we know a number of factors related to attention can vary between individuals, and some or all of these may be related to academic achievement, though in complex and interconnected ways. However, these individual differences are to a large extent outside our control, and this is important to accept.

Recent interest in "brain training" indicates a desire to overcome some of these individual differences. The idea is that with practice, we can change our working memory capacity, processing speed, and/or attentional control. Based on early results suggesting this might be possible (Klingberg, Forssberg, & Westerberg, 2002), commercial companies created brain training products and promoted them with unsubstantiated claims (Andrews, 2016). Unfortunately, all the users of these games can really expect is an improvement in their performance on the games themselves; transfer from the games to real-life tasks involving attention and working memory has not been found consistently in the research (Melby-Lervåg & Hulme, 2013).

For this reason, we prefer not to focus on these questionable interventions – instead, we focus on effective learning strategies that have decades of consistent research behind them (Weinstein, Madan, & Sumeracki, 2018; see Chapters 8 through 10).

CHAPTER SUMMARY

Attention is often defined as a "limited-capacity resource." As with a financial budget, you have a certain amount of attention, and you apportion it to different tasks. An important feature of our attentional mechanism is being able to selectively focus on just one location, object, or message at any one time. Importantly, the data point strongly to the conclusion that it is almost impossible to pay attention to more than one thing at the same time. In an educational context, not paying attention can severely impede learning. The extent to which students pay attention in educational settings depends on internal and external factors, some of which are within the instructor's control.

REFERENCES

Anderson, B. (2011). There is no such thing as attention. *Frontiers in Psychology, 2*, 246.

Andrews, J. (2016). We must challenge any company that claims to tackle dementia. *Nursing Standard, 30,* 32–32.

Baddeley, A. (2003). Working memory: Looking back and looking forward. *Nature Reviews Neuroscience, 4,* 829–839.

Baddeley, A. D., & Hitch, G. (1974). Working memory. *Psychology of Learning and Motivation, 8,* 47–89.

Bull, R., & Johnston, R. S. (1997). Children's arithmetical difficulties: Contributions from processing speed, item identification, and short-term memory. *Journal of Experimental Child Psychology, 65,* 1–24.

Chandler, P., & Sweller, J. (1991). Cognitive Load Theory and the format of instruction. *Cognition & Instruction, 8,* 293–240.

Chang, S. L., & Ley, K. (2006). A learning strategy to compensate for cognitive overload in online learning: Learner use of printed online materials. *Journal of Interactive Online Learning, 5,* 104–117.

Cohen, J., Hansel, C. E. M., & Sylvester, J. D. (1956). Mind wandering. *British Journal of Psychology, 47,* 61–62.

Deci, E. L., Koestner, R., & Ryan, R. M. (1999). A meta-analytic review of experiments examining the effects of extrinsic rewards on intrinsic motivation. *Psychological Bulletin, 125,* 627–688.

Deci, E. L., Koestner, R., & Ryan, R. M. (2001). Extrinsic rewards and intrinsic motivation in education: Reconsidered once again. *Review of Educational Research, 71,* 1–27.

Edmiston, R. W., & Braddock, R. W. (1941). A study of the effect of various teaching procedures upon observed group attention in the secondary school. *J. Educ. Psychol., 32,* 665. doi: 10.1037/h0062749

Ericsson, K. A., & Chase, W. G. (1982). Exceptional memory: Extraordinary feats of memory can be matched or surpassed by people with average memories that have been improved by training. *American Scientist, 70,* 607–615.

Feng, S., D'Mello, S., & Graesser, A. C. (2013). Mind wandering while reading easy and difficult texts. *Psychonomic Bulletin & Review, 20,* 586–592.

Forster, S., & Lavie, N. (2009). Harnessing the wandering mind: The role of perceptual load. *Cognition, 111,* 345–355.

Forster, S., & Lavie, N. (2014). Distracted by your mind? Individual differences in distractibility predict mind wandering. *Journal of Experimental Psychology: Learning, Memory, and Cognition, 40,* 251–260.

Gathercole, S. E., Pickering, S. J., Knight, C., & Stegmann, Z. (2004). Working memory skills and educational attainment: Evidence from national curriculum assessments at 7 and 14 years of age. *Applied Cognitive Psychology, 18,* 1–16.

Gopher, D., Armony, L., & Greenshpan, Y. (2000). Switching tasks and attention policies. *Journal of Experimental Psychology: General, 129,* 308–339.

Hidi, S., & Harackiewicz, J. M. (2000). Motivating the academically unmotivated: A critical issue for the 21st century. *Review of Educational Research, 70,* 151–179.

Hidi, S., Weiss, J., Berndorff, D., & Nolan, J. (1998). The role of gender, instruction and a cooperative learning technique in science education across formal and informal settings. In *Interest and learning: Proceedings of the Seeon conference on interest and gender* (pp. 215–227). Kiel, Germany: IPN.

Jackson, J. D., & Balota, D. A. (2012). Mind-wandering in younger and older adults: Converging evidence from the sustained attention to response task and reading for comprehension. *Psychology and Aging, 27,* 106–119.

James, W. (1890). *The principles of psychology* (Vol. 1). New York: Holt.

Kail, R., & Salthouse, T. A. (1994). Processing speed as a mental capacity. *Acta Psychologica, 86,* 199–225.

Kane, M. J., & Engle, R. W. (2003). Working-memory capacity and the control of attention: The contributions of goal neglect, response competition, and task set to Stroop interference. *Journal of Experimental Psychology: General, 132,* 47–70.

Klingberg, T., Forssberg, H., & Westerberg, H. (2002). Training of working memory in children with ADHD. *Journal of Clinical and Experimental Neuropsychology, 24,* 781–791.

Lavie, N., Hirst, A., De Fockert, J. W., & Viding, E. (2004). Load theory of selective attention and cognitive control. *Journal of Experimental Psychology: General, 133,* 339–354.

Ling, J., Heffernan, T. M., & Muncer, S. J. (2003). Higher education students' beliefs about the causes of examination failure: A network approach. *Social Psychology of Education, 6,* 159–170.

Loisette, A. (1896). *Assimilative memory, or, how to attend and never forget.* New York and London: Funk & Wagnalls Company.

Mayer, R. E., & Moreno, R. (2003). Nine ways to reduce cognitive load in multimedia learning. *Educational Psychologist, 38,* 43–52.

McVay, J. C., & Kane, M. J. (2009). Conducting the train of thought: Working memory capacity, goal neglect, and mind wandering in an executive-control task. *Journal of Experimental Psychology: Learning, Memory, and Cognition, 35,* 196–204.

McVay, J. C., & Kane, M. J. (2012). Why does working memory capacity predict variation in reading comprehension? On the influence of mind wandering and executive attention. *Journal of Experimental Psychology: General, 141,* 302–320.

Melby-Lervåg, M., & Hulme, C. (2013). Is working memory training effective? A meta-analytic review. *Developmental Psychology, 49,* 270.

Moray, N. (1967). Where is capacity limited? A survey and a model. *Acta Psychologica, 27,* 84–92.

Mrazek, M. D., Phillips, D. T., Franklin, M. S., Broadway, J. M., & Schooler, J. W. (2013). Young and restless: Validation of the Mind-Wandering Questionnaire (MWQ) reveals disruptive impact of mind-wandering for youth. *Frontiers in Psychology, 4.*

Pashler, H. (1999). *The psychology of attention.* Cambridge, MA: MIT Press.

Reason, J. T., & Mycielska, K. (1982). *Absent minded? The psychology of mental lapses and everyday errors.* Englewood Cliffs, NJ: Prentice Hall.

Reiss, S. (2012). Intrinsic and extrinsic motivation. *Teaching of Psychology, 39,* 152–156.

Risko, E. F., Anderson, N., Sarwal, A., Engelhardt, M., & Kingstone, A. (2012). Everyday attention: Variation in mind wandering and memory in a lecture. *Applied Cognitive Psychology, 26,* 234–242.

Roebers, C. M. (2006). Developmental progression in children's strategic memory regulation. *Swiss Journal of Psychology, 65,* 193–200.

Rotgans, J. I., & Schmidt, H. G. (2011). The role of teachers in facilitating situational interest in an active-learning classroom. *Teaching and Teacher Education, 27,* 37–42.

Schupak, C., & Rosenthal, J. (2009). Excessive daydreaming: A case history and discussion of mind wandering and high fantasy proneness. *Consciousness and Cognition, 18,* 290–292.

Smallwood, J., & Schooler, J. W. (2006). The restless mind. *Psychological Bulletin, 132,* 946–958.

Smallwood, J., Fishman, D. J., & Schooler, J. W. (2007). Counting the cost of an absent mind: Mind wandering as an underrecognized influence on educational performance. *Psychonomic Bulletin & Review, 14*(2), 230–236.

Smallwood, J., McSpadden, M., & Schooler, J. W. (2008). When attention matters: The curious incident of the wandering mind. *Memory & Cognition, 36,* 1144–1150.

Smallwood, J., Fitzgerald, A., Miles, L. K., & Phillips, L. H. (2009). Shifting moods, wandering minds: Negative moods lead the mind to wander. *Emotion, 9,* 271–276.

Stawarczyk, D., Majerus, S., Catale, C., & D'Argembeau, A. (2014). Relationships between mind-wandering and attentional control abilities in young adults and adolescents. *Acta Psychologica, 148,* 25–36.

Sweller, J., & Chandler, P. (1994). Why some material is difficult to learn. *Cognition and Instruction, 12,* 185–233.

Tapola, A., Veermans, M., & Niemivirta, M. (2013). Predictors and outcomes of situational interest during a science learning task. *Instructional Science, 41,* 1047–1064.

Teasdale, J. D., Dritschel, B. H., Taylor, M. J., Proctor, L., Lloyd, C. A., Nimmo-Smith, I., & Baddeley, A. D. (1995). Stimulus-independent thought depends on central executive resources. *Memory & Cognition, 23,* 551–559.

Wang, Z., & Duff, B. R. (2016). All loads are not equal: Distinct influences of perceptual load and cognitive load on peripheral ad processing. *Media Psychology, 19,* 589–613.

Weinstein, Y. (2018). Mind-wandering, how do I measure thee with probes? Let me count the ways. *Behavior Research Methods, 50,* 642–661.

Weinstein, Y., Madan, C. R., & Sumeracki, M. A. (2018). Teaching the science of learning. *Cognitive Research: Principles and Implications, 3,* 1–17.

Everything you do requires memory in some form or another.

"Memory is not like a library (or a computer); memory is reconstructive."

We don't lay down objective, definitive memory traces that are later retrieved verbatim.

Every time you retrieve a memory, you reconstruct it, activate it, and may alter it.

The fact that memory is reconstructive necessarily means that memory is not objective.

Details from your imagination can become part of your memories

Multiple processes are thought to make up the rich experience that we call memory.

When cognitive psychologists talk about short-term memory, they are talking about a very brief (15–30 seconds) period of time.

As soon as you encode something, you immediately start to forget it.

MEMORY

Memory is used in almost any everyday activity. But as soon as we learn something, we immediately start to forget it.

INTRODUCTION TO MEMORY: WHY IS IT SO IMPORTANT?

Ah, memory. I (Yana) am feeling dreamy as I type this, because memory is my greatest love. Memory is the reason why I'm a cognitive psychologist. Both of us (Yana and Megan) are passionate about memory, and have dedicated most of our adult lives so far to examining how our human memory works. But why?

Well, think about your life. Think about how you define yourself, who you are. Maybe you see yourself as a hard worker. That might be because for many years you have proven yourself through working hard, and you *remember* working hard a lot.

Maybe you think of yourself as a parent. That conjures up *memories* of your child's birth, or adoption, or first bruise that you blamed yourself for, or first day at school when you couldn't believe they were already that old.

Maybe you think of yourself as kind and helpful to others, and immediately *remember* that time you drove over to your best friend's house in the middle of the night to deal with an emergency.

Your very identity is most likely full of things you remember yourself doing. Maybe you also have an identity that is aspirational, partly projected into the future, full of lofty goals – "I will get my bachelor's degree," "I will start my own business," "I will retire and live in Florida" – but what do we do when we imagine this future? There has been a flurry of research into "future mental time-travel," and the leading theory is that it involves more or less the same processes as remembering (Szpunar, Watson, & McDermott, 2007). What we're actually doing when we're envisaging our future might involve taking bits and pieces of things we've experienced – be it in our own lives, in books, or in movies – and splicing them together to form a new imagined situation (Botzung, Denkova, & Manning, 2008).

But our self-concept is not the only thing we need our memory for. Actually, we would argue that *everything you do requires memory in some form or another.*

Everything you do requires memory in some form or another.

That might seem like an extreme statement, but here are some examples. Note that these are just a few specific examples, and in no way do they encompass all of the ways in which we rely on memory!

- **Remembering names.** Some of us might say we are "bad with names," but ultimately most of us find that some people's names – such as those of the members of our family – are much easier to bring to mind (Bahrick, Bahrick, & Wittlinger, 1975). This is because we've had many opportunities to practice using those names over and over again.

when you park it in the same lot every day (da Costa Pinto & Baddeley, 1991).

- **Remembering to do something in the future.** *Prospective memory* allows us to be able to plan to do something, like take a pill at a certain time in the future, and this particular type of memory is strongly affected in older age (Brandimonte, Einstein, & McDaniel, 1996).

- **Remembering whether we've done something.** Has this ever happened to you? You go to take your medicine, but you can't remember whether you've already taken it … uh oh. The process that prevents us from being sure is called *interference* (Insel, Morrow, Brewer, & Figueredo, 2006) and is a very common and serious problem for people (especially older adults) who tend to be on more medications and tend to have poorer memories.

- **Remembering where something is.** This is another case where interference comes up in everyday life: for example, remembering where you parked your car on a given day,

- **Being able to comprehend speech.** When you are listening to someone speak, you have to integrate the words they are saying one after the other, as you do not hear them simultaneously. If you instantly forgot each word as soon as you heard it, you would just hear a set of individual words that would not come together to create understanding (this is known as the Transient Information Effect; Leahy & Sweller, 2011). The process we use for this type of in-the-moment sense-making is called *working memory* (Daneman & Merikle, 1996; see Chapter 6).

- **Remembering *how* to do something.** Sometimes, you're able to remember a procedure or set of actions without really being able to describe it. For example, you can

play the piano, hit the perfect volley in tennis, or you're much faster at typing. These skills all require a form of memory, too. This skill-based memory is sometimes called procedural memory (Squire, 1987), as compared to declarative memory, which involves being able to report one's memories. The infamous amnesic patient H. M. showed us that even when our declarative memory fails – that is, we cannot describe our memories – implicit memory may remain intact (Gabrieli, Milberg, Keane, & Corkin, 1990).

And yet, despite this rich variety of functions, memory has recently come under fire. Some claim that now that we have the internet, we no longer need to worry about memory. While there's a lot of hype about the internet replacing our memory, humans have actually been relying on external memory systems for years. Books contain a wealth of information and have been around for centuries, and we've been writing memos for ourselves (notes, lists, and reminders) for many, many generations; one does not need to be a "digital native" in order to use external memory resources adaptively (Loh & Kanai, 2016).

Having said that, a fascinating line of research is now examining the cognitive consequences to these behaviors, called "cognitive offloading" (Risko & Gilbert, 2016). For example, one set of studies showed that in some situations, we are more likely to forget something we took a picture of than something we just looked at (Henkel, 2014).

We recently came across the following question, which alludes to the declining importance of human memory: "Ask yourself, why don't I just use my computer?" The answer to that question should be obvious: because you can't use a computer without using your memory first. We might be adapting from remembering information to remembering *how to obtain* that information from external sources (Sparrow, Liu, & Wegner, 2011) – but that still requires memory!

So, if almost everything we do requires memory, then most certainly this is going to be an important concept to understand with regards to learning. With that in mind, let's take a look at what is currently known about memory.

MEMORY IS NOT LIKE A LIBRARY (OR A COMPUTER) – MEMORY IS RECONSTRUCTIVE

Memory is not like a library (or a computer); memory is reconstructive.

Early on, before cognitive psychologists started researching the processes involved, memory was often described with a "library" analogy. This is the idea that memories are put down in our minds as though they were written down in books and stored away neatly in organized locations. If we wanted to retrieve a memory, we would go down the relevant aisle and select the appropriate book. If we can't quite retrieve the memory, the words printed in the books may have faded with time, and if we can't find the memory at the specified location, perhaps it was like a library book getting misplaced.

But many studies have shown that this is not at all the way memory functions. We don't lay

> *We speak of **storing** memories, of **searching** for and **locating** them. We **organize** our thoughts; we **look** for memories that have been **lost**, and if we are fortunate, we **find** them.* (1980, p. 232)

Henry Roediger

down objective, definitive memory traces that are later retrieved verbatim. Instead, memory is reconstructive (Schacter, 2015).

We don't lay down objective, definitive memory traces that are later retrieved verbatim.

This is a key concept in long-term memory: the idea that every time you retrieve a memory, you are actually changing it.

Every time you tell the same story, it comes out a little more polished, with a few embellishing details added, or a few boring ones removed. The memory itself – not just the story – is changing, so that the next time you retrieve the memory of that event, it will be more like the story you last told, rather than the way it really was. Memory

Every time you retrieve a memory, you reconstruct it, activate it, and may alter it.

is reconstructive in nature, and every time a memory is activated, it is altered.

Here's a concrete example of memory reconstruction, first demonstrated almost 100 years ago (Bartlett, 1995 [1932]).

In this demonstration, one person was shown an ambiguous drawing (in the top left of the picture). This person was then asked to try to reproduce the drawing from memory. Because we like to classify things into categories rather than dealing with unknown objects (Smith & Medin, 1981), the person who was trying to draw the ambiguous original drawing from memory drew it to look kind of like an owl. Their drawing was then shown to another person, who again was asked to reproduce it from memory, and this cycle continued. As you can see, the drawing gradually evolved from an owl to a cat! Each time someone re-drew the picture from memory, they changed it, and eventually even the animal itself changed.

MEMORY IS NOT OBJECTIVE

The fact that memory is reconstructive necessarily means that memory is not objective. Our memories are a lot more approximate and less accurate than you might like to believe. In particular, we are prone to having "false" memories – these are memories of things that never happened or happened quite differently to the way we remember them (Loftus & Pickrell, 1995). In addition, since we see the world through our own unique filter – our world view – we tend to remember things in a way that fits our "schema," or pre-determined categorizations of the world and how objects and people behave (Tversky & Marsh, 2000).

The idea that we can have memories that are "false" gained credibility starting in the 1970s and was a topic of hot debate for decades after that. The leader of this field is Dr. Elizabeth Loftus, who demonstrated that eyewitness testimony can be inadvertently affected by information encountered after the event ("misleading post-event information"). Imagine you are a witness to a crime. It was dark, but you think you saw a tall man in a mask, holding something in his hand. After this event, you are questioned repeatedly by the police, and you also discuss the event over and over with your friend who was standing next to you when this happened.

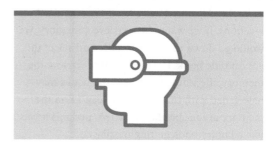

The fact that memory is reconstructive necessarily means that memory is not objective.

Elizabeth Loftus revolutionized our understanding of how eyewitness testimony works. She demonstrated in numerous experiments that by the time you've had all those conversations with the police and your friend, your memory of the crime in the above story will have become a mixture of (a) what you actually saw, (b) what you told people you saw, and (c) what other people told you they saw or think you should have seen.

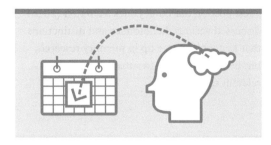

Details from your imagination can become part of your memories.

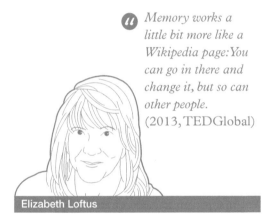

❝ *Memory works a little bit more like a Wikipedia page: You can go in there and change it, but so can other people.* (2013, TEDGlobal)

Elizabeth Loftus

So, for instance, if you were asked over and over about a weapon, you might come to imagine one and believe that the suspect really was carrying a weapon, even if your original memory of the event did not include a weapon. The details from your imagination will become part of the new memory for the event.

Similar reconstructive memory effects can also occur in an educational context. Often, we will remember the information itself along with the source it came from. But, according to the Source Monitoring Framework (Johnson, Hashtroudi, & Lindsay, 1993), it is possible to misattribute memories to incorrect sources. For example, if your friend tells you something, you later might believe you heard it from your teacher, or another reliable source.

I (Megan) have a false or distorted memory of burning my hand when I was a child. It did happen, but I do not remember it accurately: I picture it in the house I grew up in and remember, whereas this actually happened in the house we lived in up until I was four, and I can't remember that house at all.

Even details from our dreams can make it into our memories of real-life events (Johnson, Kahan, & Raye, 1984). When I was 11, I (Yana) once dreamed that my chamber music lesson was canceled, and didn't bring my music to school that day because I had confused the dream with real life. I am not sure my teacher believed my excuse at the time.

So, we have seen that recalling information in a reconstructive way can potentially introduce errors. On the other hand, understanding that memories are reconstructed each time we retrieve them is important as it underpins some of the strategies we discuss in Part 3 of the book. In particular, recalling information *correctly* actually strengthens memory (see Chapter 10).

MEMORY CONSISTS OF MANY DIFFERENT PROCESSES

Aside from being reconstructive and subjective, memory is also not a unitary process. Instead, multiple processes are thought to make up the rich experience that we call memory. In a guest post on our blog, James Mannion (2016) discussed various dichotomies and distinctions that frequently come up in memory research, but here we focus on two that are particularly relevant to education.

When cognitive psychologists talk about short-term memory, they are talking about a very brief (15–30 seconds) period of time.

Multiple processes are thought to make up the rich experience that we call memory.

Short-term vs. long-term memory

Have you heard people referring to how they can never find stuff they've left around the house, and following this with "my short-term memory is really bad"? That would be a scientifically inaccurate use of that term. When cognitive psychologists talk about short-term memory, they are really just talking about a very brief (roughly 15–30 seconds) period of time. The reason why cognitive psychologists believe that there is something truly special about the 15–30 second range that can be separated from all other memory beyond that time frame is that patients who present with apparently total memory loss are still able to keep things in memory for 15–30 seconds.

William James wrote a book in 1890 – *Principles of Psychology* – which, unlike cognitive psychology, was based entirely on his own intuitions – or, more formally, introspections – rather than experiments and data. Even before

any data were gathered to support the idea of a distinction between short- and long-term memory, William James proposed it – although he referred to the two types of memory as primary memory (things that you are holding in your memory right now) and secondary memory (everything else, stuff that you remember for longer than just in the moment).

The first patient to demonstrate a profound loss of long-term memory along with perfectly intact short-term memory was called H.M. He was treated for epilepsy when he was in his 20s; since this was the 1950s and they didn't know any better, the doctors removed part of his brain as an attempt to cure him of his seizures. This did result in improvement in terms of epilepsy, but with huge consequences: H.M. also lost the ability to form new long-term memories – at least, those that he could report (i.e., declarative memories). For the 40 years that he lived after his surgery, he didn't form any meaningful new memories about his life.

If asked what he ate for breakfast that day, H.M. didn't know, and if asked when he started suffering from memory loss (yes, he knew that something was wrong), he would say maybe a year ago, regardless of how many decades had passed. Each time he saw the researcher that would test him probably at least once a week for those 40 years, he introduced himself anew.

This is all to say that despite how severely his long-term memory was affected, his short-term memory remained just as good as mine, or yours. That is, if you read out a phone number to H.M., he could repeat it back to you just as well as the next person. This also explains why

H.M. was actually able to hold relatively normal-seeming conversations, as long as the subject did not extend beyond the present situation.

H.M. died in 2008, and the researcher who had studied him for his entire post-operative life has published a book about him. In this book, Corkin describes memory as if it were a hotel, with short-term memory represented by the lobby, and long-term memory represented by the guest rooms.

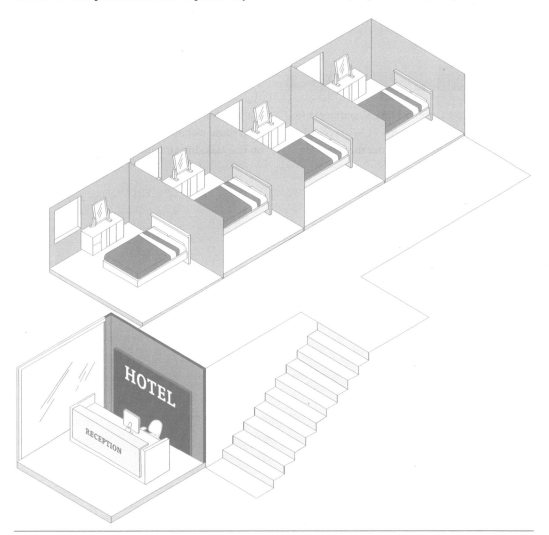

Information passes through short-term memory, but it doesn't stay for long, and there's a limit to the amount of information that can fit in.

Here is what Corkin says about H.M.:

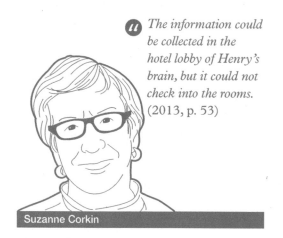

> **❝** *The information could be collected in the hotel lobby of Henry's brain, but it could not check into the rooms.* (2013, p. 53)

Suzanne Corkin

To illustrate how sensitive H.M.'s memory is to this distinction between short- (15–30 seconds) and long-term memory, consider the following

experiment (Prisko, 1963). H.M. was shown two shapes, one after the other, and his job was to indicate whether the shapes were the same, or different. The length of time between presentation of the two shapes varied between 15 and 60 seconds. Here are examples of same and different shape pairs:

We will first describe how control participants (i.e., those without memory loss) would perform on this task. Imagine that there are 12 trials

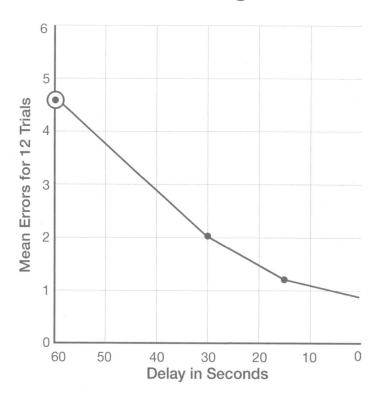

in the experiment: six where the pairs are the same, and six where they are different. If you were randomly guessing, you might expect to get about half of them correct. A typical adult will only get on average one of the 12 trials wrong (getting 11/12 correct) when the first and second shapes are presented 60 seconds apart.

Now, what about H.M.? His data appear on the graph below.

The dot to the far right, above the 0, demonstrates that when the shapes were presented at the same time (as they are in the example above!), H.M. was pretty good at determining whether they were the same or different. He only made one error in 12 trials. When the shapes were presented 15 seconds apart, he was still pretty good at the task (the mean error displayed on the graph is between one and two trials, because these data were aggregated across five different versions of the task).

But once the delay was increased beyond 30 seconds, there was a sharp rise in the number of errors H.M. made, and by the time the delay was 60 seconds, it was as if he was randomly guessing. Recall that the average normal participant only makes one error when the shapes are 60 seconds apart; this is not a difficult task. What this shows is that while H.M. could keep the first shape in his memory for about 15–30 seconds, beyond that the memory faded away, and he was no longer able to compare it to the second shape and make an accurate decision about whether they were the same or different.

Procedural vs. declarative memory

The kind of memory that we usually think of when we talk about memory in everyday life is *declarative memory*. This refers to memories that we can directly access, voluntarily report the contents of, and are aware of remembering. After his operation, H.M. wasn't able to do

many of the things we described at the beginning of the chapter: learning a new person's name, remembering whether he had taken a pill, or where he had placed an object.

However, it is not exactly accurate to say that H.M. was unable to form long-term memories. In fact, H.M. did have a partially intact long-term memory! This is evidenced by the fact that he was able to learn to use a walker, able to do the myriad cognitive tasks that researchers subjected him to for decades, and more generally, able to rely on his memory *as long as he was not explicitly asked to report its contents* (Corkin, 2013).

Procedural memory is demonstrated in your actions, and does not involve directly reporting the contents of one's memory. Examples of procedural memory include things that you can do without thinking about how to do them, such as walking; and things you can do without being able to explain how you did them, such as finding your way home from a certain location without being able to tell me the directions. H.M. still had access to this memory process after his operation.

The following task cleverly demonstrates the difference between procedural and declarative memory. In the first version of the task, H.M. would be shown a list of words, such as CLAY, CALCIUM, ROUGH, etc. Then (at least 30 seconds later, once short-term memory had been cleared, because – remember – he had an intact short-term memory), he would be presented with "word stems." These word stems were the first three letters of each studied word, such as "CLA-," "CAL-," and "ROU-." His job was to complete the word stems with words he had just seen.

Note that these instructions described above explicitly referred H.M. back to the study phase of the experiment. H.M. performed very poorly on this task, because it required him to report on the contents of his memory.

In the procedural version of the task, everything was exactly the same except the test instructions. This time, instead of being asked to complete the word stems with previously studied words, H.M. was simply asked to come up with any random word that started with those letters. Now, all of a sudden, he performed like a healthy control participant: he was much more likely to complete the word stems with words he had studied than other (unstudied) words that could fit, even though he had no awareness that he was actually relying on his memory to perform this task.

GETTING THINGS INTO LONG-TERM MEMORY

In order for memory to be recallable later, it needs to go from short-term to long-term memory (checking into the hotel, in Corkin's analogy above). Whether something makes it from short- to long-term memory depends on a number of factors, some of which may not yet have been pinned down. However, a very important factor is whether information is encoded in a deep or meaningful way (Craik & Lockhart, 1972), so that connections can be made and understanding can be achieved. In Chapter 9, we discuss why making connections and achieving understanding is so important to learning.

Long-term memory is often talked about in terms of a four-stage model: encoding, consolidation, storage, and retrieval (Nader & Hardt, 2009). If a memory is never encoded, then it was never created in the first place, so there is nothing to retrieve (for example, imagine holding a piece of paper with a string of numbers on it right in front of your face, but with your eyes completely shut the whole time the paper is in front of you).

Just because a memory is encoded, however, does not mean that it will be recallable later; it needs to be consolidated. And, consolidation

of a memory is not a one-off event. When the memory is retrieved, it is reconstructed, reactivated, and re-consolidated (Sara, 2000).

As we discussed in Chapter 2, the majority of this book is focused on understanding learning on a cognitive level – that is, how learning takes place in the mind, rather than pin-pointing specific biological processes in the brain that lead to learning. However, I (Yana) recently had coffee with Efrat Furst, who was trained as a cognitive neuroscientist, and now translates this research for educators.

In Furst's opinion, there are some basics that all learners and teachers should understand about how memory functions – not just on the cognitive level, but also on the neuroscientific level. Current research is moving us closer and closer to connecting these levels (Hardt, Einarsson, & Nader, 2010), though it's important to note that for now, these two levels are not completely integrated (Coltheart, 2006).

HOW IS MEMORY REPRESENTED IN THE BRAIN? BY EFRAT FURST

From a neuroscientific perspective, memory is everything that one has ever experienced and is represented in the neuronal networks of the brain: simple or complex, conscious or unconscious, facts, events, procedures, and so on. In educational contexts, however, memory is sometimes disregarded as "just memory" in contrast to other, more sophisticated forms of knowledge. But for brain scientists, there are no other forms of knowledge: everything that is learned is memory. The important questions to ask are "how is memory represented?" and" how might this influence future behavior?" Our unique and enormous long-term memory store is what makes each of us an individual. However, the principles of how memory is stored in the brain are common among us all, and therefore valuable to everyone – and to educators in particular.

Here are the basic neuroscientific principles, as they are currently understood, that guide my thinking about learning and memory:

1. **How are memories represented in the brain?**

   The brain is made of nerve-cells, or neurons, that communicate with each other: an active neuron may activate another neuron if they have a mutual connection (synapse) that is strong enough. Memories are represented by groups of neurons that are connected to each other by synapses. When active neurons in a certain group are synchronously active, we are able to recall a concept or an episode, or to execute a procedure. Neuroscientists call this pattern of active neurons an "*engram*". Engrams can be connected to one another (by synapses) to create associations. One specific memory can be composed of multiple engrams, sometimes in different anatomical locations, that are connected to each other by neuronal **pathways**. Engrams,

associations, and pathways are all made of out neurons with synapses between them. This is a common way to represent a highly simplified network of neurons (e.g., Tonegawa, Liu, Ramirez, & Redondo, 2015).

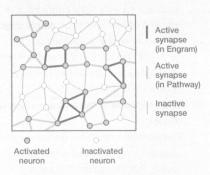

Active synapse (in Engram)

Active synapse (in Pathway)

Inactive synapse

Activated neuron   Inactivated neuron

2. **What happens when we learn?**

   When we learn something new, specific groups of neurons are firing in our brain as a response to the incoming information, creating patterns. Some of these patterns are absolutely new; others represent things that we already know. The crucial question is: will these first-time-ever-active patterns be reproducible in the future? We know that in order to remember, we need to reactivate a highly similar pattern to the one that was active during learning (but without the original stimulus; Tonegawa *et al.*, 2015). But what does this depend on?

3. **How does newly acquired information turn into engrams and get stored in the brain?**

   Under certain conditions, a network that was just active (while learning) is undergoing **consolidation**: connections between the just-active neurons are strengthened to create an engram. This process takes energy, time, and biological resources, and is required to create a long-lasting engram (reviewed in Dudai, 2004). Rest and sleep are known to play an important part in consolidation (reviewed in Dudai, Karni, & Born, 2015). Consolidation is crucial not just for the creation of the engrams, but also to create the neuronal pathways leading to them and their associations with other engrams. It is also known that having an established network of prior knowledge (or "schema") makes it easier and faster to consolidate new memories (Tse *et al.*, 2007; Gilboa & Marlatte, 2017).

4. **What happens to the engram when we use it?**

Following consolidation, memories are officially "long-term memories", which implies that we can use the same memory over and over again for long periods of time. However, some neuroscientific findings challenge this notion in interesting and important ways (Nader & Hardt, 2009). It turns out that consolidation is not a one-time event. Rather, following activation upon retrieval, the engrams become malleable and subject to subsequent modification by **re**consolidation. This understanding has crucial implications: after every retrieval attempt, the activated engrams, as well as the activated associations and pathways, stand a chance to undergo reconsolidation. It means that every time we use them, we are reconstructing our network of memories.

Neuroscience of Retrieval

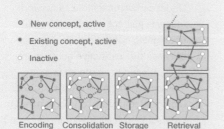

New concept, active

Existing concept, active

Inactive

Encoding   Consolidation   Storage   Retrieval

Putting it all together (and extending the scientific findings to create a full picture): it is crucial to remember that construction and reconstruction processes are dependent on simultaneous activity: neurons that "fire together wire together" (e.g. Hebb, 1949; Tse *et al.*, 2007). When we learn a new concept, its retention depends on constructing the engram and on forming associations with existing engrams. This, in turn, depends on our ability to retrieve the existing engrams and create the connections actively when learning.

THE COGNITIVE SCIENCES AND THE NEUROSCIENCES

These principles are valuable as a basis for considering several strategies that are known to be effective for learning, on the basis of work from the cognitive sciences. In a way, the neuroscientific evidence allows us to think more concretely about the possible underlying mechanisms and understand the benefits of spacing out practice (Chapter 8), creating meaningful connections between new and prior knowledge (Chapter 9), and retrieving prior knowledge (Chapter 10). These strategies allow new information to be integrated with retrieved prior knowledge, and then consolidated. This effortful reconstruction process is the key to an effective learning experience.

FORGETTING

Arguably, one of the most important features of memory is actually the opposite of remembering: forgetting. This fundamental concept has been explored for well over 100 years (first starting with Ebbinghaus (1913), whom you will encounter in Chapter 8), yet researchers have still not reached a consensus on the exact definition of the term.

An extreme form of forgetting would be the total obliteration of any memory trace; no evidence of this pure form of forgetting has yet been found (Davis, 2008). More realistically, we might think about forgetting as the inability to remember something that you once knew (Tulving, 1974).

Have you ever studied something – for example, learned some vocabulary in a foreign language – and reached a certain level of proficiency, only to find yourself completely incapable of remembering the words you thought you had once mastered? What has happened to this knowledge that you had before? You might say that you have "forgotten" it – but what does that really mean?

What you are experiencing is an inability to retrieve information after it was once learned – in other words, a retrieval failure. As such, we should be able to overcome retrieval failure by providing hints or "retrieval cues." Tulving and Pearlstone (1966) demonstrated the effectiveness of providing hints by having participants try to remember a list of 48 words – two words from each of 24 categories, such as "articles of clothing: blouse, sweater" and "types of birds: blue jay, parakeet." On the later test, participants were either just asked to write down as many words as they could remember, or they were provided with hints or cues in the form of the category names (e.g., "articles of clothing: ?). Providing these retrieval cues increased memory output from 40 percent of the words to 75 percent, suggesting that most of the words that appeared to be "forgotten" could still be retrieved with additional cues.

One thing we do know about forgetting is that it starts immediately after encoding, and happens quite rapidly before slowing down.

The graphs on the following page, often called "forgetting curves," demonstrate how much information is retained when people are tested on it at different amounts of time post-learning (technically, these are actually retention curves as they show the amount of information decreasing; see Roediger, Weinstein, & Agarwal,

As soon as you encode something, you immediately start to forget it.

2010). Regardless of what window of time we are interested in, the forgetting function is always going to look similar. On the following page you will find two examples of "forgetting curves" from different time frames.

The rest of this book is dedicated to mitigating against forgetting in an academic context. In Chapter 8, we will learn about how to space studying over time in order to interrupt the steep forgetting curve. In Chapter 9, we will discuss how to deepen understanding, which is essential for learning. And finally, in Chapter 10 we will discuss how bringing information to mind from memory can stimulate the re-consolidation process and strengthen learning

CHAPTER SUMMARY

Early on, before cognitive psychologists started researching the processes involved, memory was often described with a "library" analogy. This is the idea that memories are put down in our minds as though they were written down in books, and stored away neatly in organized locations. If we wanted to retrieve a memory, we would go down the relevant aisle and select the appropriate book. If we can't quite retrieve the memory, the words printed in the books may have faded with time, and if we can't find the memory at the specified location, perhaps it was like a library book getting misplaced. But is this analogy a good one? In this chapter, we discuss how human memory really works, and why this is important for teachers to know.

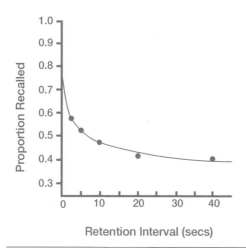
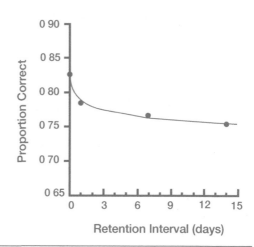

These graphs represent the proportion of information retained either over the course of 40 seconds (word recall) or two weeks (face recognition). Based on Experiments 1 and 2 of Wixted and Ebbesen (1991).

REFERENCES

Bahrick, H. P., Bahrick, P. O., & Wittlinger, R. P. (1975). Fifty years of memory for names and faces: A cross-sectional approach. *Journal of Experimental Psychology: General, 104,* 54–75.

Bartlett, F. C. (1995 [1932]). *Remembering: A study in experimental and social psychology.* Cambridge: Cambridge University Press.

Botzung, A., Denkova, E., & Manning, L. (2008). Experiencing past and future personal events: Functional neuroimaging evidence on the neural bases of mental time travel. *Brain and Cognition, 66,* 202–212.

Brandimonte, M., Einstein, G. O., & McDaniel, M. A. (Eds.) (1996). *Prospective memory: Theory and applications,* Mahwah, NJ: Erlbaum.

Coltheart, M. (2006). What has functional neuroimaging told us about the mind (so far)? *Cortex, 42,* 323–331.

Corkin, S. (2013). *Permanent present tense: The unforgettable life of the amnesic patient, H.M.* New York: Basic Books.

Craik, F. I., & Lockhart, R. S. (1972). Levels of processing: A framework for memory research. *Journal of Verbal Learning and Verbal Behavior, 11,* 671–684.

da Costa Pinto, A. A. N., & Baddeley, A. D. (1991). Where did you park your car? Analysis of a naturalistic long-term recency effect. *European Journal of Cognitive Psychology, 3,* 297–313.

Daneman, M., & Merikle, P. M. (1996). Working memory and language comprehension: A meta-analysis. *Psychonomic Bulletin & Review, 3,* 422–433.

Davis, M. (2008). Forgetting: Once again, it's all about representations. *Science of Memory: Concepts,* 317–320.

Dudai, Y. (2004). The neurobiology of consolidations, or, how stable is the engram? *Annu. Rev. Psychol., 55,* 51–86.

Dudai, Y., Karni, A., & Born, J. (2015). The consolidation and transformation of memory. *Neuron, 88,* 20–32.

Ebbinghaus, H. (1913). *Memory: A contribution to experimental psychology* (No. 3). University Microfilms.

Gabrieli, J. D., Milberg, W., Keane, M. M., & Corkin, S. (1990). Intact priming of patterns despite impaired memory. *Neuropsychologia, 28,* 417–427.

Gilboa, A., & Marlatte, H. (2017). Neurobiology of schemas and schema-mediated memory. *Trends in Cognitive Sciences, 21,* 618–631.

Hardt, O., Einarsson, E. Ö., & Nader, K. (2010). A bridge over troubled water: Reconsolidation as a link between cognitive and neuroscientific memory research traditions. *Annual Review of Psychology, 61,* 141–167.

Hebb, D. O. (1949). *The organization of behavior.* New York: Wiley.

Henkel, L. A. (2014). Point-and-shoot memories: The influence of taking photos on memory for a museum tour. *Psychological Science, 25,* 396–402.

Insel, K., Morrow, D., Brewer, B., & Figueredo, A. (2006). Executive function, working memory, and medication adherence among older adults. *The Journals of Gerontology Series B: Psychological Sciences and Social Sciences, 61,* 102–107.

James, W. (1890). *The principles of psychology* (Vol. 1). New York: Holt.

Johnson, M. K., Hashtroudi, S., & Lindsay, D. S. (1993). Source monitoring. *Psychological Bulletin, 114*, 3–28.

Johnson, M. K., Kahan, T. L., & Raye, C. L. (1984). Dreams and reality monitoring. *Journal of Experimental Psychology: General, 113*, 329–344.

Leahy, W., & Sweller, J. (2011). Cognitive load theory, modality of presentation and the transient information effect. *Applied Cognitive Psychology, 25*, 943–951.

Loftus, E. F., & Pickrell, J. E. (1995). The formation of false memories. *Psychiatric Annals, 25*, 720–725.

Loh, K. K., & Kanai, R. (2016). How has the Internet reshaped human cognition? *The Neuroscientist, 22*, 506–520.

Mannion, J. (2016, December). GUEST POST: Learning is multidimensional — Embrace the complexity! *The Learning Scientists*. Retrieved from www.learningscientists.org/blog/2016/12/6-1

Nader, K., & Hardt, O. (2009). A single standard for memory: The case for reconsolidation. *Nature Reviews Neuroscience, 10*, 224–234.

Prisko, L. H. (1963). *Short-term memory in focal cerebral damage*, PhD Thesis, McGill University, Quebec. Canada.

Risko, E. F., & Gilbert, S. J. (2016). Cognitive offloading. *Trends in Cognitive Sciences, 20*, 676–688.

Roediger, H. L. (1980). Memory metaphors in cognitive psychology. *Memory & Cognition, 8*, 231–246.

Roediger, H. L., Weinstein, Y., & Agarwal, P. K. (2010). Forgetting: Preliminary considerations. In S. Della Sala, (Ed.), *Forgetting* (pp. 1–34). Brighton, U.K.: Psychology Press.

Sara, S. J. (2000). Retrieval and reconsolidation: Toward a neurobiology of remembering. *Learning & Memory, 7*, 73–84.

Schacter, D. L. (2015). Memory: An adaptive constructive process. In D. Nikulin (Ed.), *Memory in recollection of itself*. New York: Oxford University Press.

Smith, E. E., & Medin, D. L. (1981). *Categories and concepts.* Cambridge, MA: Harvard University Press.

Sparrow, B., Liu, J., & Wegner, D. M. (2011). Google effects on memory: Cognitive consequences of having information at our fingertips. *Science, 333*(6043), 776–778.

Squire, L. R. (1987). *Memory and brain.* New York: Oxford University Press.

Szpunar, K. K., Watson, J. M., & McDermott, K. B. (2007). Neural substrates of envisioning the future. *Proceedings of the National Academy of Sciences, 104*, 642–647.

TED. (2013, June 11). Elizabeth Loftus: The fiction of memory [Video file]. Retrieved from: https://protect-us.mimecast.com/s/J6-7COYEZrupwqnMps ELrWz?domain=blog.ted.com" https://blog.ted.com/tk-elizabeth-loftus-at-tedglobal-2013/

Tonegawa, S., Liu, X., Ramirez, S., & Redondo, R. (2015). Memory engram cells have come of age. *Neuron, 87*, 918–931.

Tse, D., Langston, R. F., Kakeyama, M., Bethus, I., Spooner, P. A., Wood, E. R., ... & Morris, R. G. (2007). Schemas and memory consolidation. *Science, 316*(5821), 76–82.

Tulving, E. (1974). Cue-dependent forgetting: When we forget something we once knew, it does not necessarily mean that the memory trace has been lost; it may only be inaccessible. *American Scientist, 62*, 74–82.

Tulving, E., & Pearlstone, Z. (1966). Availability versus accessibility of information in memory for words. *Journal of Verbal Learning and Verbal Behavior, 5*, 381–391.

Tversky, B., & Marsh, E. J. (2000). Biased retellings of events yield biased memories. *Cognitive Psychology, 40*, 1–38.

Wixted, J. T., & Ebbesen, E. B. (1991). On the form of forgetting. *Psychological Science, 2*, 409–415.

Part 3

STRATEGIES FOR EFFECTIVE LEARNING

INTRODUCTION

Researchers have made significant advances in applying cognitive processes to education.

However, few teachers encounter effective learning strategies from cognitive psychology in their training.

Each of the six strategies we discuss has received decades of support from cognitive psychology.

One
Spaced practice

Two
Retrieval practice

Three
Interleaving

Four
Elaboration

Five
Concrete examples

Six
Dual coding

INTRODUCTION

Strategies for effective learning

Researchers have made significant advances in applying cognitive processes to education (see Dunlosky, Rawson, Marsh, Nathan, & Willingham [2013] and Weinstein, Madan, & Sumeracki [2018] for reviews).

Researchers have made significant advances in applying cognitive processes to education.

From this work, recommendations can be made for students to maximize their learning efficiency (Pashler *et al.*, 2007). Specifically, six key learning strategies from cognitive research have been consistently found to be effective, and can be broadly applied to education (see Table on the next page).

However, a recent report from the US (Pomerance, Greenberg, & Walsh, 2016) as well as ongoing follow-up studies from Europe (Surma, Vanhoyweghen, Camp, & Kirschner, in prep) found that few teacher-training textbooks and courses cover these principles, and current study-skills courses also lack coverage of these important learning strategies (see Chapter 1).

However, few teachers encounter effective learning strategies from cognitive psychology in their training.

Students are therefore missing out on mastering techniques that they could use on their own to learn effectively. Thus, we've dedicated the rest of this book to unpacking each of these strategies, and providing the reader with tips on how to use them.

Each of the six strategies we discuss has received decades of support from cognitive psychology.

Learning Strategy	Description	Application Examples (using childhood development from Introduction to Psychology)
Spaced practice (Ch 8)	Creating a study schedule that spreads study activities out over time.	Students can block off time to study and restudy key concepts such as attachment styles and developmental milestones on multiple days before an exam, rather than repeatedly studying these concepts right before the exam.
Interleaving (Ch 8)	Switching between topics while studying.	After studying emotional development, students can switch to cognitive development and then to social development; next time, students can study the three in a different order, noting what new connections they can make between them.
Elaboration (Ch 9)	Asking and explaining why and how things work.	Students can explain how and why our memory changes across the lifespan: why don't we remember many things from when we were under five? How does our ability to remember change as we get older?
Concrete examples (Ch 9)	When studying abstract concepts, illustrating them with specific examples.	Students can imagine the following example to explain childhood amnesia: Two siblings, aged nine and four, go to Disney World. Ten years later, the nine-year-old remembers this trip, whereas the four-year-old does not.
Dual coding (Ch 9)	Combining words with visuals.	Students can sketch the different phases in an attachment styles study, e.g., for secure attachment style: (1) mother in room with baby, who is exploring toys; (2) mother leaves, baby is a bit upset but not inconsolable; (3) mother is back and baby happily hugs mother.
Retrieval practice (Ch 10)	Bringing learned information to mind from long-term memory.	When studying attachment styles, students can practice writing out from memory the description of a child's behavior as described by each style.

We have organized the six strategies into three chapters to follow how a student might approach studying: planning when to study (Chapter 8), developing understanding (Chapter 9), and reinforcing knowledge (Chapter 10).

Each of the six strategies we discuss has received decades of support from cognitive psychology (Dunlosky *et al.*, 2013; Pashler *et al.*, 2007; Weinstein *et al.*, 2018), though two of them have received the most: spacing, and retrieval practice.

Spacing involves distributing studying over time (Benjamin & Tullis, 2010) rather than cramming studying before an exam, which is the more

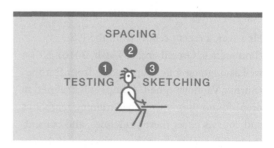

Spaced practice

common behavior among students (Weinstein, Lawrence, Tran, & Frye, 2013).

Retrieval practice involves bringing information to mind from memory, which is a technique that is much more effective at promoting long-term learning than the more common technique of re-reading class materials (Roediger & Karpicke, 2006). While students do sometimes test themselves, it is usually to check their knowledge rather than to produce learning (Karpicke, Butler, & Roediger, 2009).

Retrieval practice

Since these two strategies have received the most support from the cognitive literature, we dedicate separate chapters to each of them (Chapter 8 on Planning and Chapter 10 on Reinforcement).

The remaining four strategies - interleaving, elaboration, concrete examples, and dual coding - can be used to support spaced practice and retrieval practice.

Interleaving

Interleaving involves switching between ideas or types of problems (e.g., in math and physics), rather than studying one idea or type of problem for too long; this encourages better discrimination between ideas and procedures (Taylor & Rohrer, 2010). We've included this strategy in the chapter on Planning (Chapter 8).

Elaboration – specifically, elaborative interrogation – involves students asking (and attempting to answer) "how" and "why" questions (Pressley, McDaniel, Turnure, Wood, & Ahmad, 1987).

Elaboration

Concrete examples help students grasp abstract ideas (Paivio, 1971).

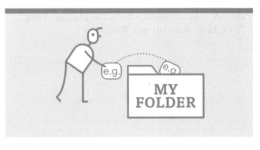

Concrete examples

Finally, dual coding combines words and visuals, giving students two pathways by which to retrieve information later (Paivio, 2007).

Dual coding

Those last three strategies help to develop understanding, so we've written about them all together in Chapter 9. Whether you are a teacher, a student, a parent, or simply interested in learning – we hope you'll find a new strategy to try out.

REFERENCES

Benjamin, A. S., & Tullis, J. (2010). What makes distributed practice effective? *Cognitive Psychology*, *61*, 228–247.

Dunlosky, J., Rawson, K. A., Marsh, E. J., Nathan, M. J., & Willingham, D. T. (2013). Improving students' learning with effective learning techniques: Promising directions from cognitive and educational psychology. *Psychological Science in the Public Interest*, *14*, 4–58.

Karpicke, J. D., Butler, A. C., & Roediger, H. L. (2009). Metacognitive strategies in student learning: Do students practise retrieval when they study on their own? *Memory*, *17*, 471–479.

Paivio, A. (1971). *Imagery and verbal processes*. New York: Holt, Rinehart and Winston.

Paivio, A. (2007). *Mind and its evolution: A dual coding theoretical approach*. Mahwah, NJ: Erlbaum.

Pashler, H., Bain, P. M., Bottge, B. A., Graesser, A., Koedinger, K., McDaniel, M., & Metcalfe, J., (2007). *Organizing instruction and study to improve student learning: IES practice guide*. Washington DC, USA: National Center for Education Research, Institute of Education Sciences, US Department of Education.

Pomerance, L., Greenberg, J., & Walsh, K. (2016, January). *Learning about learning: What every teacher needs to know*. Retrieved from www.nctq.org/dmsView/Learning_About_Learning_Report

Pressley, M., McDaniel, M. A., Turnure, J. E., Wood, E., & Ahmad, M. (1987). Generation and precision of elaboration: Effects on intentional and incidental learning. *Journal of Experimental Psychology: Learning, Memory, and Cognition*, *13*, 291–300.

Roediger, H. L., & Karpicke, J. D. (2006). Test-enhanced learning: Taking memory tests improves long-term retention. P*sychological Science*, *17*, 249–255.

Surma, T., Vanhoyweghen, K., Camp, K., & Kirschner (in prep). *Distributed practice and retrieval practice: The coverage of learning strategies in Flemish and Dutch teacher education textbooks.*

Taylor, K., & Rohrer, D. (2010). The effects of interleaved practice. *Applied Cognitive Psychology*, *24*, 837–848.

Weinstein, Y., Madan, C. R., & Sumeracki, M. A. (2018). Teaching the science of learning. *Cognitive Research: Principles and Implications*, *3*(2), 1–17.

Weinstein, Y., Lawrence, J. S., Tran, N., & Frye, A. A. (2013, November). *How and how much do student study? Tracking study habits with the diary method*. Poster presented at the annual meeting of the Psychonomic Society, Toronto, Canada.

Investigations into spaced practice date back to the late 1800s, with Ebbinghaus studying a list of syllables.

The benefits of spaced practice to learning are an important contribution of cognitive psychology to education.

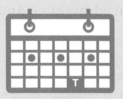

The effectiveness of spaced practice depends on the delay to the final test.

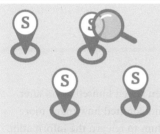

Spaced practice has been investigated in many different subjects and learning contexts.

ACB | CBA | BCA

Interleaving is another strategy that can help with planning when and what to study.

There has recently been a lot of interest in interleaving for mathematics.

ACB | CBA | BCA

The cognitive processes behind the effectiveness of interleaving are still under debate.

Outside the lab, it is very difficult to disentangle the benefits of interleaving versus spacing.

Getting students to use spaced practice is really hard. It might be difficult for them to stick to a schedule.

PLANNING LEARNING

Spaced practice and interleaving

Students often cram before exams; this "works" in a sense that they can remember the information required for the exam – but not for long. Spaced practice and interleaving are harder and less intuitive than cramming, but produce better long-term results.

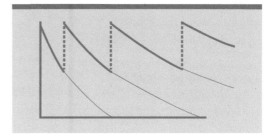

Investigations into spaced practice date back to the late 1800s, with Ebbinghaus studying a list of syllables.

SPACED PRACTICE

At the core of it, spaced practice is a very simple idea. Let's think about how students tend to get ready for exams. Many students do what we call "cramming" – that is, they might stay up all night before the exam, or maybe spend a day or two before the exam looking over their notes and trying to cram them all into memory so that they can regurgitate them in the exam. Spaced practice is the opposite of that. Instead of reading and re-reading right before the exam, spaced practice builds in opportunities to look over the material and practice it for *weeks* before the exam.

Investigations of spaced practice date back to the late 1800s, when the German researcher Hermann Ebbinghaus examined his own ability to learn and retain nonsense syllables such as TPR, RYI, and NIQ over time.

Here's how he did it: He first read a list of nonsense syllables, then tried to recite it perfectly. Of course, he couldn't get it right every time. To determine how long it took him to learn the list, Ebbinghaus counted the number of attempts it took for him to get a perfect

recitation. He then tested himself again after various delays, and counted how many more attempts it took him to relearn the information after each break, and how that differed depending on his practice schedule. After a number of years testing himself on different study schedules, Ebbinghaus concluded the following:

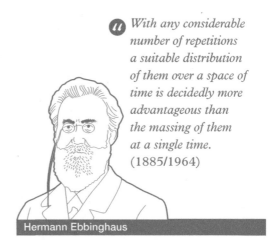

" With any considerable number of repetitions a suitable distribution of them over a space of time is decidedly more advantageous than the massing of them at a single time. (1885/1964)

Hermann Ebbinghaus

Spacing out studying over time is more effective for long-term learning than cramming study right before the exam.

Since then, the field has replicated the effect of spacing originally demonstrated in this case study in many different controlled studies, both in the laboratory and in the classroom and with children of many different ages (see Carpenter, Cepeda, Rohrer, Kang, & Pashler [2012] and Kang [2016] for reviews).

The benefits of spaced practice to learning are an important contribution of cognitive psychology to education.

But the important thing about spaced practice is that its effectiveness depends on the delay between the study session(s) and the final test or exam. If the exam is happening immediately after studying, then by all means students can read and re-read really quickly, cramming as much as they can into memory. In this case, they'll probably be able to remember some of the information in the exam, but as soon as the exam is over, that information is going to fly out of the brain as quickly as it flew in. With spaced practice, on the other hand, information is going to stick around for longer. We typically see the benefits of spaced practice after a bit of a delay, such as one or two days – rather than on an immediate test.

In one set of laboratory studies, Rawson and Kintsch (2005) had students read lengthy scientific texts. Students either read the text one time, or they read it twice in a row, or twice with a week delay in between. Then, half of the students in the experiment took an immediate test, and the other half came back two days later to take a test. The test in this study simply asked the students to write out everything they could remember from one particular section of the lengthy text (see opposite).

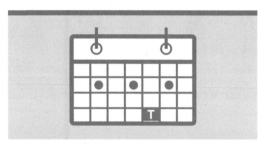

The effectiveness of spaced practice depends on the delay to the final test.

The results were strikingly different depending on whether students took an immediate test, or came back after two days (see over).

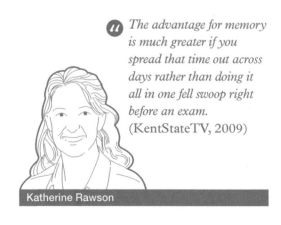

❝ The advantage for memory is much greater if you spread that time out across days rather than doing it all in one fell swoop right before an exam.
(KentStateTV, 2009)

Katherine Rawson

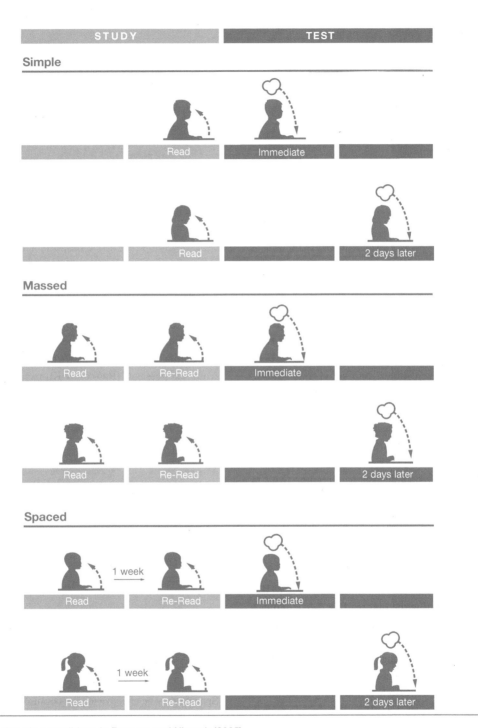

STUDY	TEST

Simple

Read — Immediate

Read — 2 days later

Massed

Read — Re-Read — Immediate

Read — Re-Read — 2 days later

Spaced

Read — 1 week — Re-Read — Immediate

Read — 1 week — Re-Read — 2 days later

The six learning conditions in Rawson and Kintsch (2005).

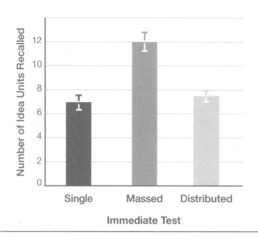
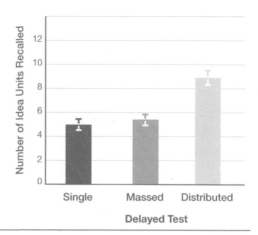

Graphs showing the effect of massing and spacing reading on immediate versus delayed tests. Data from Rawson and Kintsch (2005).

On the immediate test, it looked as though massing studying (that is, reading the text twice in a row) was the most effective strategy – better than reading just once, and better than reading twice one week apart, which looked the same as reading only once. But on the test two days later, this pattern was reversed: now, reading twice one week apart was much more effective than just reading once, or reading twice in a row. Importantly, on a delayed test, reading twice in a row was not significantly better than reading just once. So, a student studying for an exam that is in a couple of days is wasting time by reading and re-reading a chapter.

There is one caveat to the finding above. Of course, if a student is not fully attending to the material during the first reading (see Chapter 6 on Attention) then they may get something extra out of reading a second time right away. Not all initial readings are the same. However, all other things being equal, continuing to read and re-read ultimately is not going to produce as much long-term durable learning as is spacing these reading opportunities over time.

Spaced practice has been investigated in many different subjects and learning contexts, from

simple vocabulary learning (Bahrick, Bahrick, Bahrick, & Bahrick, 1993), fact learning (DeRemer & D'Agostino, 1974), and learning from text passages (Rawson & Kintsch, 2005), to problem solving (Cook, 1934), motor skills (Baddeley & Longman, 1978), and learning to play a musical instrument (Simmons, 2012).

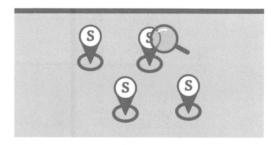

Spaced practice has been investigated in many different subjects and learning contexts.

Spacing may be effective in part because it increases what some researchers call "storage strength" – a measure of deep learning – rather than our current ability to produce information (known as "retrieval strength"; Bjork & Bjork, 1992).

Storage strength indexes learning and, once accumulated, is never lost. (Bjork, 2013)

Bob Bjork

INTERLEAVING: ANOTHER PLANNING TECHNIQUE

ACB | CBA | BCA

Interleaving is another strategy that can help with planning when and what to study.

If we forget a little before we restudy information, this allows us to boost that storage strength when we re-encounter the information. To learn more about retrieval and storage strength, read the excellent guest blog post by Veronica Yan (Yan, 2016).

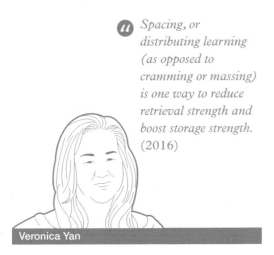

Spacing, or distributing learning (as opposed to cramming or massing) is one way to reduce retrieval strength and boost storage strength. (2016)

Veronica Yan

Another strategy that can help with planning when and what to study is called interleaving. For a student, that would involve taking the ideas you are trying to learn, and mixing them up – or, switching between ideas and varying the order in which they are practiced. Rather than studying very similar information in one study session, you might take things that are somewhat related but not too similar, and mix things up by studying those ideas in various orders (see over).

To what extent is this technique effective? The research on interleaving spans many domains – some more relevant to everyday learning than others: motor learning, musical instrument practice, and mathematics, to name a few. Motor learning studies typically involve having participants learn different keystroke patterns either by practicing the same pattern over and over (blocked practice), or by switching between different patterns (interleaved practice).

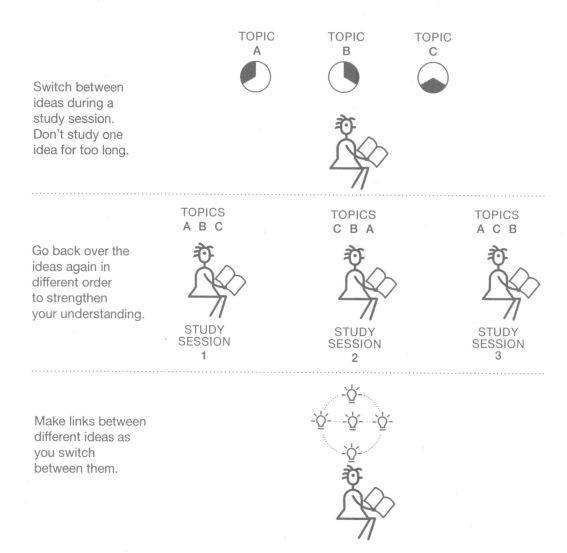

Switch between ideas during a study session. Don't study one idea for too long.

Go back over the ideas again in different order to strengthen your understanding.

Make links between different ideas as you switch between them.

Typically, interleaved practice produces poorer accuracy and speed during learning, but improved accuracy and speed on a later testing session compared to blocked practice (Shea & Morgan, 1979). This extends to motor learning outside of the lab, too: for example, golf coaches familiar with the cognitive literature recommend interleaved practice of different golf swings (Lee & Schmidt, 2014), and of course this would apply to any other sport. For example, in one study, children were shown to improve their beanbag-tossing skills after interleaved practice compared to blocked practice (Carson & Wiegand, 1979).

More relevant to academic learning, there has recently been a lot of interest in interleaving for mathematics.

In studies looking at interleaving in math, typically students are given a variety of math skills to learn, and are given practice on these skills either blocked by skill, or interleaved so

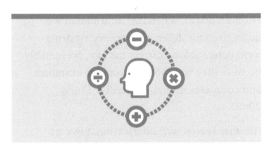

There has recently been a lot of interest in interleaving for mathematics.

(Rohrer & Taylor, 2007) – all with the same results: while students perform better on the blocked task during learning, the opposite is true on a later test, and dramatically so. For example, in a study with 4th graders, students were taught how to use different formulas to calculate different features of three-dimensional objects: faces, edges, etc. They then practiced either doing many of the same type of problem in a row, or switching between those different formulas (see below).

In the blocked condition, students' performance dropped from 100 percent to 38 percent in just one day, whereas those in the interleaved condition maintained their performance from 81 percent during learning to 78 percent a day later (Taylor & Rohrer, 2010) (see over).

that various different skills are practiced in one session. This design has been implemented with students in elementary school (Taylor & Rohrer, 2010), middle school (Rohrer, Dedrick, & Burgess, 2014), and college

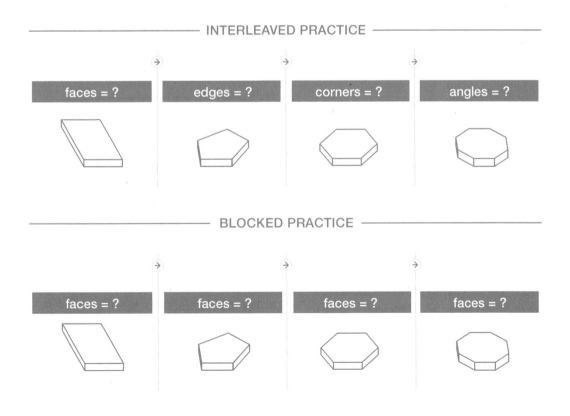

INTERLEAVED PRACTICE

faces = ?   edges = ?   corners = ?   angles = ?

BLOCKED PRACTICE

faces = ?   faces = ?   faces = ?   faces = ?

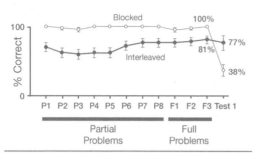

This figure shows performance during practice (P1 through F3) and on the test the next day. P1 through P8 refers to practice trials where the formula was provided for students who had to apply it to solving each problem. F1 to F3 refers to practice trials where the formula was no longer provided and students had to recall it to solve each problem. This was also the case on the test.

WHY DOES INTERLEAVING WORK?

The cognitive processes behind the effectiveness of interleaving are still under debate.

The cognitive processes behind the effectiveness of interleaving are still under debate. Some have argued that interleaving allows the learner to better distinguish between different concepts; additional evidence for this comes from inductive learning experiments in which students had to extract learning from a series of pieces of information about a concept

(Rohrer, 2012). When this information was intermixed for different concepts, students were better able to extract the gist, presumably because they were able to compare examples and counterexamples (Kornell & Bjork, 2008).

Another reason why interleaving might be helpful – particularly for problem-solving subjects – is that it forces the learner to retrieve the right *strategy* to answer each different type of problem that they encounter. This is helpful because (a) it mirrors real life, where we do not typically get to answer a lot of similar questions in a row, and (b) because it allows the learner to select incorrect strategies and make errors that can then be corrected; this helps students to understand which strategy is used in which situations.

THE FUTURE OF INTERLEAVING

Despite the striking results highlighted in the previous section, there is still a lot we don't know about interleaving, making it much more difficult for us to recommend how it should be implemented by teachers and learners. First of all, we don't yet know exactly what type of material should be interleaved. While we know that interleaving completely different things, like science concepts and foreign language vocabulary, is not terribly helpful (Hausman & Kornell, 2014), we don't know what level of similarity is ideal. We also don't know what interleaving does to attention (see Chapter 6): it could hurt attention to the extent that interleaving is similar to multi-tasking, but it could also improve attention to the extent that switching between topics may reduce boredom and mind-wandering.

Another issue with interleaving is that outside of very contrived laboratory studies, it is very difficult to disentangle the benefits of

Outside of the lab, it is very difficult to disentangle the benefits of interleaving versus spacing.

interleaving from those obtained by spaced practice.

That is, imagine that you are interleaving by practicing material you learned today, together with material you learned last week. That involves interleaving, but by bringing back information from last week, you're now also doing spaced practice! As such, we recommend teachers focus more on spaced practice than interleaving – but keeping in mind that during each individual study session, it could be helpful to mix up studying different ideas or answering different types of problems, especially if students will need to be able to distinguish between them later on.

SPACED PRACTICE IN THE CLASSROOM

We are thrilled to see the changes currently being implemented by real teachers in classrooms across the world. Here are a few examples from teachers implementing spacing in the classroom.

- Mr. Benney (Benney, 2016) writes on his blog about how he staggers math homework assignments on a given topic by one month, and then teaches a review session a month later (and a few months later as well, for topics studied earlier in the academic year). This encourages students to keep information in mind as they learn it, rather than compartmentalizing it after each topic is covered.

- Mr. Tharby (Tharby, 2014), an author and teacher in the UK, starts each of his classes by asking the students to review older material by giving small quizzes. He asks the students three questions about information from the

TOPIC	SEP	OCT	NOV	DEC	JAN	FEB	MAR	APR	MAY	JUN
1	Taught	Lag Hwk		SL 1				SL 2		
2		Taught	Lag Hwk		SL 1			SL 2		
3			Taught		Lag Hwk	SL 1			SL 2	
4				Taught		Lag Hwk		SL 1		
5					Taught	Lag Hwk			SL 2	
6						Taught	Lag Hwk		SL 2	
7								Taught	Lag Hwk	
8									Taught	

Spacing table from Mr. Benney's (2016) blog post.

last class, one question about information from the last week, one question about information from the last month, and then finally asks one question that requires the students to make a link between information from the last class and something learned earlier. By asking students these questions, he is spacing out when the students are thinking about the information already taught. This exercise also combines spacing with retrieval practice, a beneficial learning strategy that we discuss in Chapter 10.

Getting students to use spaced practice is really hard. It might be difficult for them to stick to a schedule.

We should end by acknowledging that helping students to plan out when they will study is hard.

In fact, I (Yana) have an anecdote about this very issue. In May 2017, I was planning on giving a talk in French at the University of Toulouse. I had never given a talk in French before (I do speak French, but hadn't done so in a work context before that point). About six weeks out from my talk, I was trying to think about when I would prepare for it. My instinct – believe it or not! – was to set aside two whole days right before the talk. Essentially, to just cram the whole thing. This felt very efficient to me.

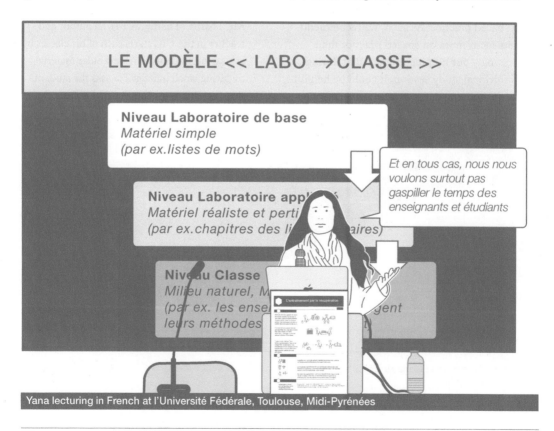

Yana lecturing in French at l'Université Fédérale, Toulouse, Midi-Pyrénées

But as I was about to block off that time in my schedule, I suddenly came to my senses: I was planning to prepare for a talk about spaced practice … by cramming. Quickly realizing my mistake, I decided to set aside 30 minutes per day for the next six weeks (coincidentally, that's a total of about 21 hours, or two full days of work) to practice the talk. I blocked off 30 minutes per day on my calendar, choosing a timeslot in the late morning that was usually open on any given day. What do you think happened every day when that time block came around? Well, some days I was too engrossed in what I was already doing, or quite frankly too lazy to study my French talk. It seemed so far away – there were six weeks, then five weeks, then four weeks still to go … but on other days, I did follow my own instructions and pulled out the presentation to practice. At the very least, I did this a lot more than I would have without having time-blocked the study sessions.

In Part 4, we give further tips for teachers who want to help their students plan out their studying.

CHAPTER SUMMARY

The benefit of spaced practice to learning is arguably one of the strongest contributions that cognitive psychology has made to education. The effect is simple: repetitions spaced out over time will lead to greater retention of information in the long run than the same number of repetitions close together in time. Interleaving is another planning technique that can increase learning efficiency. Interleaving occurs when different ideas or problem types are tackled in a sequence, as opposed to the more common method of attempting multiple versions of the same problem in a given study session (known as blocking). More research is needed to fully understand how and when interleaving works. Spaced practice, in the meantime, is ready to be implemented in the classroom and at home.

REFERENCES

Baddeley, A. D., & Longman, D. J. A. (1978). The influence of length and frequency of training session on the rate of learning to type. *Ergonomics, 21,* 627–635.

Bahrick, H. P., Bahrick, L. E., Bahrick, A. S., & Bahrick, P. E. (1993). Maintenance of foreign language vocabulary and the spacing effect. *Psychological Science, 4,* 316–321.

Benney, D. (2016, October 16). (Trying to apply) spacing in a content heavy subject [Blog post]. Retrieved from https://mrbenney.wordpress.com/2016/10/16/trying-to-apply-spacing-in-science/

Bjork, R. A. (2013, October 11). Forgetting as a friend of learning: Implications for teaching and self-regulated learning. Talk presented at William James Hall. Retrieved from https://hilt.harvard.edu/files/hilt/files/bjorkslides.pdf

Bjork, R. A., & Bjork, E. L. (1992). A new theory of disuse and an old theory of stimulus fluctuation. In A. Healy, S. Kosslyn, & R. Shiffrin (Eds.), *From learning processes to cognitive processes: Essays in honor of William K. Estes* (Vol. 2, pp. 35–67). Hillsdale, NJ: Erlbaum.

Carpenter, S. K., Cepeda, N. J., Rohrer, D., Kang, S. H., & Pashler, H. (2012). Using spacing to enhance diverse forms of learning: Review of recent research and implications for instruction. *Educational Psychology Review, 24,* 369–378.

Carson, L. M., & Wiegand, R. L. (1979). Motor schema formation and retention in young children: A test of Schmidt's schema theory. *Journal of Motor Behavior, 11,* 247–251.

Cook, T. W. (1934). Massed and distributed practice in puzzle solving. *Psychological Review, 41,* 330–355.

DeRemer, P., & D'Agostino, P. R. (1974). Locus of distributed lag effect in free recall. *Journal of Verbal Learning and Verbal Behavior, 13,* 167–171.

Ebbinghaus, H. (1885/1964). *Memory: A contribution to experimental psychology.* Mineola, NY: Dover Publications.

Hausman, H., & Kornell, N. (2014). Mixing topics while studying does not enhance learning. *Journal of Applied Research in Memory and Cognition, 3,* 153–160.

Kang, S. H. (2016). Spaced repetition promotes efficient and effective learning. *Policy Insights from the Behavioral and Brain Sciences, 3,* 12–19.

KentStateTV (2009). Dr. Katherine Rawson speaks about her research [YouTube video]. Retrieved from www.youtube.com/watch?v=ZeJXCpCsIbk

Kornell, N., & Bjork, R. A. (2008). Learning concepts and categories: Is spacing the "enemy of induction"? *Psychological Science, 19,* 585–592.

Lee, T. D., & Schmidt, R. A. (2014). PaR (Plan-act-Review) golf: Motor learning research and improving golf skills. *International Journal of Golf Science, 3,* 2–25.

Rawson, K. A., & Kintsch, W. (2005). Rereading effects depend on time of test. *Journal of Educational Psychology, 97,* 70–80.

Rohrer, D. (2012). Interleaving helps students distinguish among similar concepts. *Educational Psychology Review, 24,* 355–367.

Rohrer, D., & Taylor, K. (2007). The shuffling of mathematics problems improves learning. *Instructional Science, 35*(6), 481–498.

Rohrer, D., Dedrick, R. F., & Burgess, K. (2014). The benefit of interleaved mathematics practice is not limited to superficially similar kinds of problems. *Psychonomic Bulletin & Review, 21,* 1323–1330.

Shea, J. B., & Morgan, R. L. (1979). Contextual interference effects on the acquisition, retention, and transfer of a motor skill. *Journal of Experimental Psychology: Human Learning and Memory, 5,* 179–187.

Simmons, A. L. (2012). Distributed practice and procedural memory consolidation in musicians' skill learning. *Journal of Research in Music Education, 59,* 357–368.

Taylor, K., & Rohrer, D. (2010). The effects of interleaved practice. *Applied Cognitive Psychology, 24,* 837–848.

Tharby, A. (2014, June). Memory platforms [Blog post]. *Reflecting English Blog.* Retrieved from https://reflectingenglish.wordpress.com/2014/06/12/memory-platforms/

Yan, V. (2016, May). Retrieval strength versus storage strength [Blog post]. *The Learning Scientists Blog.* Retrieved from www.learningscientists.org/blog/2016/5/10-1

Elaboration describes the process of adding features to one's memories.

For understanding to happen, new information needs to be connected to pre-existing knowledge.

Understanding can be increased through strategies that promote elaboration.

Elaborative interrogation involves asking and answering "how" and "why" questions.

Concrete examples help illustrate abstract ideas and make them easier to understand.

It is important to use multiple concrete examples to illustrate abstract concepts.

Pictures are generally remembered better than words, and can provide an additional memory cue.

Combining pictures with words can be helpful for all learners – not just those who like pictures.

Any pictures accompanying written material must be relevant to target concepts.

DEVELOPMENT OF UNDERSTANDING

▬▬▬

As teachers, we hope that our students will learn material in a meaningful manner – that is, that they will understand it. Understanding occurs when students elaborate a memory by adding details to it and integrating it with existing knowledge, and can be enhanced by several effective strategies.

WHAT IS ELABORATION?

Elaboration is one of the most frequently discussed concepts among memory researchers (Smith, 2014). Likely one of the reasons elaboration is discussed at length is that the term is very broad and can mean a lot of different things. In the simplest terms, elaboration means to add something to a memory (see Hirshman, 2001; Postman, 1976).

Elaboration describes the process of adding features to one's memories.

Elaboration is also thought to encourage organization, or the connecting and integrating of ideas (Bellezza, Cheesman, & Reddy, 1977; Mandler, 1979). When new information is integrated and organized with information that

was already known, this process makes it easier to remember the new information later on.

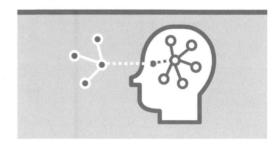

For understanding to happen, new information needs to be connected to pre-existing knowledge.

Another way of defining elaboration is to think about information on a deeper level (Craik & Lockhart, 1972; Craik & Tulving, 1975). The idea is that information can be processed at various levels. Shallow processing involves analyzing information with regard to surface details, such as indicating whether a word is written in all capital letters or whether its font is bold. Deeper processing involves thinking about the meaning of the word. Thinking deeply about meaning is thought to induce elaboration. According to this framework, one remembers information better if it is processed more deeply compared to when it is processed in a shallow manner.

Elaboration is thought to be one of the best ways to increase learning and memory among many memory theorists. For example, in 1983, Anderson said, "one of the most potent manipulations that can be performed in terms of increasing a subject's memory for material is to have the subject elaborate on the to-be-remembered material" (p. 285). If that is true,

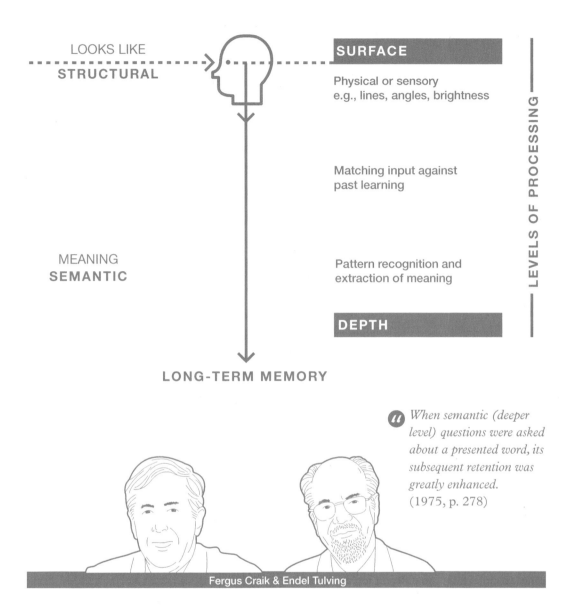

LOOKS LIKE
STRUCTURAL

SURFACE

Physical or sensory
e.g., lines, angles, brightness

Matching input against
past learning

MEANING
SEMANTIC

Pattern recognition and
extraction of meaning

LEVELS OF PROCESSING

DEPTH

LONG-TERM MEMORY

When semantic (deeper level) questions were asked about a presented word, its subsequent retention was greatly enhanced.
(1975, p. 278)

Fergus Craik & Endel Tulving

then all we as educators need to do is make sure that students are elaborating, and then they should maximize their learning! If only it were that simple.

We have spent a lot of time thinking about the idea of elaboration. (In fact, Megan's entire doctoral dissertation was all about elaboration and retrieval!) From our perspective, the idea of elaboration is so broad that it can become difficult to use in practice. Additions to memory can mean almost anything. Even more problematic is that the term has become somewhat circular: when a process is found to improve learning and memory we attribute this to elaboration, but if a process does not improve learning and memory then we conclude elaboration did not occur, or did not occur enough (Karpicke & Smith, 2012).

The term elaboration itself may be too broad to utilize effectively in educational settings. However, there are three specific techniques – elaborative interrogation, concrete examples, and dual coding – that have shown promise in improving student learning and helping students understand the material they are learning.

Elaborative interrogation involves asking and answering "how" and "why" questions.

Understanding can be increased through strategies that promote elaboration.

ELABORATIVE INTERROGATION: WHAT'S THE MAIN IDEA?

Elaborative interrogation is a specific method of elaboration where you ask yourself questions about how and why things work, and then produce the answers to those questions (McDaniel & Donnelly, 1996; Pressley, McDaniel, Turnure, Wood, & Ahmad, 1987). The specific questions to ask will depend, in part, on the learning topic at hand. Below are some examples from two different topics: neural communication, and the attack on Pearl Harbor.

Neural communication example

How does neural communication work? Well, if we look at one neuron, the dendrites receive messages from many other neurons, and then the messages converge in the soma. If there is enough of a positive charge within the soma, then an action potential will occur, and an electrical signal is sent down the axon. When the signal reaches the terminal buttons, neurotransmitters are released into the synapse where they communicate with the dendrites of the next neuron.

Why does this happen? The neurotransmitters are chemicals that allow neurons to communicate with one another. Overall, the pattern of activation among different neurons (which neurons fire, how quickly, what neurotransmitters they release) determines the message in your brain.

How does the axon work? The axon is a long tail-like structure that produces the electrical signal.

How does the signal travel? The axon is covered in myelin sheath, a fatty substance that insulates the axon. The myelin sheath works like the rubber around the cord of an electrical appliance, and it serves to make the electricity travel faster.

Why have myelin sheath? Because we need our neurons to be able to send signals quickly, since we need to be able to react quickly, make decisions quickly, move quickly, perceive feeling in our skin quickly, etc.

Pearl Harbor example

How did this attack happen? On December 7, 1941, the Imperial Japanese Navy attacked the United States Naval Base at Pearl Harbor. The attack included Japanese fighter planes, bombers, and torpedo planes.

Why did this happen? The Japanese intended to destroy the United States' Pacific Fleet so that it could not interfere with Japanese operations.

What was the result of this historic event? Well, Japanese casualties were light, while they damaged eight U.S. Navy battleships. The *Arizona* was among those that the Japanese sunk, and was not raised from the shallow water. U.S. aircraft were also destroyed, and 2,403 Americans were killed (1,178 were injured).

Why is this event important? The day after the attack, Roosevelt delivered his Infamy Speech, the United States formally declared war on Japan, and Japanese-Americans were then relocated to internment camps.

You could then go on: how did the U.S. enter the war? How did the Pearl Harbor attack lead up to the release of the atomic bomb? How did the war end? And so on.

The main goal is to ask a number of questions that encourage you (or your students) to explain the main concepts. As you are elaborating, you are making connections between old and new knowledge, making the memories easier to retrieve later. Of course, these questions are just example questions, and there are a lot of different questions one could ask. The important thing is that the questions lead to describing and explaining the main ideas, and making connections between various ideas.

This process of generating elaborative questions and finding the answers to them has been shown to be better for student learning than simply reading the information, and even having students select their own study strategies. For example, Woloshyn and Stockley (1995) had 6th and 7th grade students learn science facts that were consistent with their prior knowledge and facts that were inconsistent with their prior knowledge.

An example of a consistent or unsurprising science fact from their research is "the larger an

Vera Woloshyn

animal is, the more oxygen it needs to live." But take, for example, this fact: "the sun is made up of every color, including blue and violet." This type of fact might be more surprising to students. The study looked at how elaborative interrogation impacted learning of both types of facts. The students worked either independently, or in pairs – and in one of three learning conditions: elaborative interrogation, students' own strategy, and reading aloud (see over for a graphic with more details on each condition).

Learning was assessed both immediately and 60 days after the study session. Studying in pairs versus independently did not make a difference to later learning, but students who practiced elaborative interrogation learned more than those in the other two learning conditions. This was true both for facts that were consistent and those that were inconsistent with prior knowledge. Importantly, this learning was durable – 60 days after the study session, students who practiced elaborative interrogation still performed best.

It's interesting to note that students who selected their own study strategy did not do any better

Working alone | Working in pairs

 A

Elaborative interrogation: answering the question *"Why is that fact true?"* and using their class materials to help.

Working alone | Working in pairs

 B

Select their own study strategy: students were told to study the facts in whatever way they thought would help them learn them best, and think back to strategies that had worked in the past.

Working alone | Working in pairs

 C

Read the information for understanding, out loud.

Learning conditions in Woloshyn and Stockley's (1995) elaboration study.

than those who just read for understanding. Thus, students were better able to understand and remember the facts, even if they were inconsistent with their prior beliefs, when they used elaborative interrogation compared to other learning strategies. Importantly, these findings demonstrate another point about elaborative interrogation: it is a flexible strategy because students can do this both on their own and in groups (see also Kahl & Woloshyn, 1994).

There was one important caveat to the findings from Woloshyn and Stockley's research: the quality of the elaborative interrogation answers mattered. Students performed best when they produced an adequate response to the question. However, producing an "inadequate" response was *still* better than providing no response at all. And finally, studying in pairs did not lead to a larger number of adequate responses than did studying alone.

Other research, however, has shown that when background knowledge on the topic is low, elaborative interrogation does not help as much as when the students have high background knowledge (Woloshyn, Pressley, & Schneider, 1992). And in some cases where the quality of the elaborations produced is really poor, this process can actually hurt learning compared to additional reading (Clinton, Alibali, & Nathan, 2016). For these reasons, elaborative interrogation is best utilized by teachers to help develop understanding, not necessarily when first introducing a topic.

Not many studies have yet taken the elaborative interrogation method out of the lab and into the classroom (see Chapter 2 for the lab-to-classroom model). The one classroom study we know about, however, did find encouraging results. In this study (Smith, Holliday, & Austin, 2010), almost 300 undergraduates enrolled in a biology course were randomly assigned to re-read or answer "why" questions about information that they were studying as part of their class. The authors found a small but significant advantage for the elaborative interrogation group compared to the re-reading group, and they found this even when they controlled for prior knowledge and verbal ability. (So, it wasn't just that students with greater prior knowledge or greater verbal ability happened to be in the elaborative interrogation group.) These results are promising, and will hopefully be explored further in the near future to provide further evidence that the elaborative interrogation technique can be used effectively in the classroom.

SELF-EXPLANATION: WHAT'S THE MAIN IDEA?

Self-explanation is somewhat similar to elaborative interrogation in its function and outcomes. Self-explanation has most commonly been studied in math and physics, and involves students trying to explain the steps that they are taking out loud as they solve a problem.

Not self-explaining | Self-explaining

In a correlational study (that is, there was no experimental manipulation here), researchers found that college students who engaged in self-explanation while trying to solve physics problems showed better understanding of the concepts on a later test (Chi, Bassok,

Lewis, Reimann, & Glaser, 1989). However, the correlation between self-explanation and better understanding of the concepts on a test does not tell us that self-explanation causes better understanding (see Chapter 2). It could be that self-explaining leads to better performance on a test, but it could also be that better understanding of the material leads to both greater self-explanation and greater test performance. There could also be other factors that influence both self-explanation and test performance. (see p. 442 of Chi, de Leeuw, Chui, & LaVancher, 1994). The correlation tells us that the two are related, but does not tell us *how* they are related.

In order to determine causality, we need a true experiment. In a true experiment, random assignment is used and a variable (or multiple variables) is manipulated. Then, the outcome is measured and the researcher looks for differences caused by the manipulation. Once Chi and colleagues found the correlation between self-explanation and better understanding of the concepts, the next step was a true experiment.

In a follow-up study (Chi *et al.*, 1994), the researchers specifically prompted one group of students to self-explain, while the other group were left to do whatever they normally did (some self-explained, while others didn't). Because they randomly assigned students to be prompted to self-explain or not, this study represents a true experiment. The experimental group who were prompted to self-explain performed significantly better than the control group on a later test of understanding, suggesting self-explanation itself does lead to greater performance on a test later. Similar results were found with elementary school students learning to solve word problems in math, with better performance in the self-explanation group on both an immediate test and a test one month after initial study (Tajika, Nakatsu, Nozaki, Neumann, & Maruno, 2007).

One interesting application of the self-explanation method is the prepare-to-teach method, where you end up learning the material really well because you have to get good enough to be able to teach it to someone else. In fact, even just expecting to have to teach the material, without actually teaching it, produces great learning gains over preparing for a test (Nestojko, Bui, Kornell, & Bjork, 2014)!

CONCRETE EXAMPLES: WHAT'S THE MAIN IDEA?

Abstract ideas can be vague and hard to grasp, and humans are better able to remember concrete information than abstract information (Paivio, Walsh, & Bons, 1994). As such, concrete examples of abstract ideas can be very helpful for understanding and remembering information.

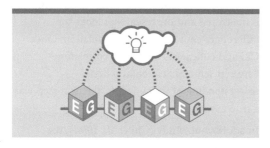

Concrete examples help illustrate abstract ideas and make them easier to understand.

Scarcity: a concrete example

Take "scarcity" as an example of an abstract idea. Scarcity can be explained as follows: *the rarer something is, the higher its value will be.* But this description contains a lot of vague terms, such as "rarer" and "value." How can we make this idea more concrete? We could use a specific example to illustrate the idea.

Think about an airline company. If you were to try to book a flight four months in advance, the ticket prices would probably be pretty reasonable. But as it gets closer to the date of travel, there will be fewer seats left on the plane (the seats are rarer). This scarcity drives up the cost (value) of the tickets. This is a concrete example of scarcity, which is an abstract idea.

Providing examples seems easy enough – and we probably all do it when we teach – but one potential problem is that students may remember the concrete example, but not remember the underlying abstract idea. In other words, students might just remember the surface details of the example and not remember the links to the underlying concept the instructor was trying to teach. (Or, possibly they never really understood the links to begin with.) We have a concrete example of this concept (pun intended).

When I (Megan) was in graduate school, the first class I taught solo was a hybrid section of Introduction to Psychology. As a way to demonstrate positive reinforcement to the class, I decided to bring in candy. I used the candy as a positive reinforcement for class participation, and (thankfully) was able to increase students' participation by giving them candy in the class. The demonstration seemed to work well in the moment.

However, at the end of the semester, when I received my course evaluations, many of the students said "I liked her class, she gave us candy." Part of me was stunned. Why didn't they realize that the candy was used to demonstrate a principle? I suppose I shouldn't have been surprised. My students remembered the surface details of the example, (i.e., there was candy) without remembering the underlying structure (i.e., positive reinforcement, for example with candy, can be used to increase a behavior, for example participation).

There is a plethora of research showing that students often notice and remember the surface details of an example rather than the underlying structure, especially as novices. For example,

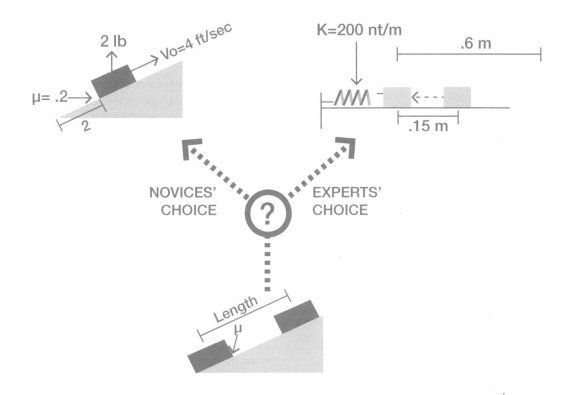

physics experts are able to extract underlying structure from problems to sort them into categories, while physics novices tended to sort problems by surface details (Chi, Feltovich, & Glaser, 1981; see Smith [2016] for a blog post describing this study).

Students seem to have trouble ignoring the surface details and focusing on the underlying structure of examples. This is especially problematic when students need to transfer what they are learning from one example to another – an important goal for education! Gick and Holyoak (1980) examined whether college students could use one problem to solve another analogous problem. First, the students read a story about a general trying to capture a fortress:

A small country was ruled from a strong fortress by a dictator. The fortress was situated in the middle of the country, surrounded by farms and villages. Many roads led to the fortress through the countryside. A rebel general vowed to capture the fortress. The general knew that an attack by his entire army would capture the fortress. He gathered his army at the head of one of the roads, ready to launch a full-scale direct attack. However, the general then learned that the dictator had planted mines on each of the roads. The mines were set so that small bodies of men could pass over them safely, since the dictator needed to move his own troops and workers to and from the fortress. However, any large force would detonate the mines. Not only would this blow up the road, but it would also destroy many neighboring villages. It seemed impossible to capture the fortress. However, the general devised a simple plan. He divided his army into small groups and dispatched each group to the head of a different road. When all was ready, he gave the signal and each group marched down a different road. Each group continued down its road to the fortress, so that the entire army arrived together at the fortress at the same time. In this way, the general captured the fortress and overthrew the dictator.

Then, after a few minutes, the students were given a couple of problems to solve, including a problem analogous to the fortress problem:

> Suppose you are a doctor faced with a patient who has a malignant tumor in his stomach. To operate on the patient is impossible, but unless the tumor is destroyed, the patient will die. A kind of ray, at a sufficiently high intensity, can destroy the tumor. Unfortunately, at this intensity, the healthy tissue that the rays pass through on the way to the tumor will also be destroyed. At lower intensities the rays are harmless to the healthy tissue, but will not affect the tumor.

> How can the rays be used to destroy the tumor without injuring the healthy tissue?

The problems have very different surface details. One includes a general, an army, a fortress, roads, and mines, while the other includes a patient, a doctor, a tumor, radiation, and healthy tissue. Yet they both have the same underlying structure, and the solution presented in the

fortress problem – break up a large force into smaller forces to converge in the middle – can be used to solve the tumor problem.

However, across a number of experiments, few students were able to spontaneously transfer the solution from one problem to the next. In one of their experiments, only 20 percent of students spontaneously solved the tumor problem using the analogous general problem. This is surprising because the two problems were presented during the same experimental session! When students were given a hint – "In solving this problem you may find that one of the stories you read before will give you a hint for a solution of this problem" – many more solved the problem (92 percent), but this means with an explicit hint 8 percent of students still could not make the connection between the two examples. Certainly, the hint scenario is not practical; how many students have a teacher following them throughout their lives giving them hints about when to apply various things they have learned?

HOW MANY CONCRETE EXAMPLES DO WE NEED?

Providing concrete examples can help students understand abstract ideas, but when teaching novices we run the risk of students remembering the surface details of the example, which isn't as

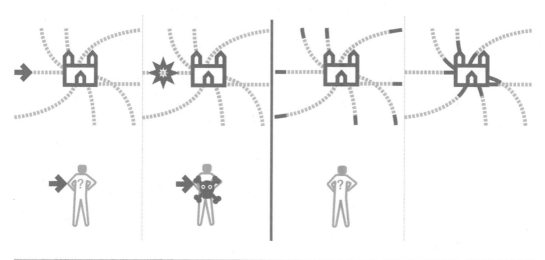

important as remembering and understanding the abstract ideas themselves. Selectively remembering only the surface details will make it extremely difficult for students to then notice and apply the abstract idea when they come across a different relevant example. One way of trying to help students understand the underlying idea is to provide students with multiple examples (Gick & Holyoak, 1983). This will be especially helpful if the various examples have different surface details.

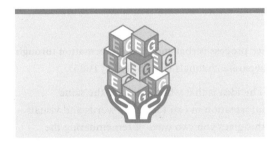

It is important to use multiple concrete examples to illustrate abstract concepts.

Take the example of scarcity from earlier in the chapter. We provided one example about buying tickets for an airline. But later, what if the students remember that what they learned had something to do with planes, but don't remember anything else? They will have missed the point of the concrete example. To help alleviate this, we could also provide an example about ticket sales for sports games. Well before the season starts tickets are more plentiful and are often less expensive. However, as the sports season progresses, and a team performs well, more people want to go see the team. Tickets become scarce as they sell – there are fewer seats available in the stadium – and as a result the remaining tickets become more expensive. This provides another concrete example of scarcity, but this example still has some surface details in common with the first example. Students may

think that scarcity has to do with ticket sales, whether for an airline or a sports game, but nothing else.

Finally, consider another very different example. In dry areas if there is a drought, then water, a natural resource, becomes scarce. In these situations, the value placed on water is higher. It can be more expensive to purchase water, and due to the lack of resources the city may even put restrictions on how much water each household is allowed to use in a given day or week. Now the value of every drop of water we use becomes greater, and we will be less likely to want to waste water on things we don't need – a drought is probably not the best time for a water balloon fight or to fill the pool – and save the water for times when we really need it, like drinking, bathing, and cooking.

The water in a drought concrete example still demonstrates the abstract idea of scarcity, but has different surface details from the airline tickets and sports game tickets examples. While the first two dealt with money and tickets, the third example is about natural resources and saving. Providing this type of range of concrete examples makes it more likely that students will be able to look past the surface details, and understand the abstract idea. To read more about why providing multiple examples is important, you can read a guest post on our blog by Althea Bauernschmidt (Bauernschmidt, 2017).

It is important to note that concrete examples do not always improve learning. In some cases, concrete examples such as physical manipulatives (i.e., objects that are used to demonstrate an abstract concept) can actually *impede* learning. This can happen if manipulatives are too fun to play with, thereby driving attention (see Chapter 6) away from the learning task; or if the surface features of the concrete examples are too salient, driving attention away from the abstract concept they are supposed to represent (McNeil, Uttal, Jarvin, & Sternberg, 2009).

Vivid concrete examples can actually *reduce* transfer in some cases, because the learner becomes so fixated on the specific features of the concrete example that they can't see the connection to the abstract idea and other examples (Carbonneau, Marley, & Selig, 2013). Overall, making connections from concrete examples to abstract ideas is difficult for those with less knowledge of the subject at hand, and instructors need to make these connections explicit for learners.

DUAL CODING: WHAT'S THE MAIN IDEA?

Dual coding is the process of combining verbal materials with visual materials. Pictures are often remembered better than words (Paivio & Csapo, 1969; 1973). Dual coding theory is the idea that when we combine text information and visual information, our learning is enhanced because

Pictures are generally remembered better than words, and can provide an additional memory cue.

we process verbal and visual information through separate channels (Paivio, 1971; 1986).

The idea is that when you have the same information in two formats – words and visuals – this gives you two ways of remembering the information later on.

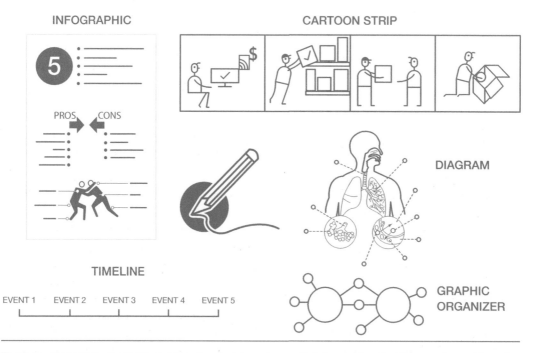

There are many ways to visually represent material, such as with infographics, timelines, cartoon strips, diagrams, and graphic organizers.

DUAL CODING VS. LEARNING STYLES

Because dual coding involves presenting information in visual and verbal form, it can start to sound like we are talking about learning styles. We already discussed misunderstandings around learning styles in Chapter 4, and noted that there is a great deal of research showing that assessing learning style and then matching instruction to style does not improve learning (see Pashler, McDaniel, Rohrer, & Bjork, 2008). We all have preferences, sure – but matching instruction to these preferences does not lead to improved learning.

Instead, dual coding suggests that, regardless of preferences, students tend to learn better when you combine modalities. For example, let's say we have a student who states that they prefer diagrams and actually need diagrams in order to learn. (Anecdotally, a lot of our students tend to tell us that they're visual learners, and thus learn best from the pictures.) The learning styles theory (Dunn, 2000) would suggest that we should only give additional visual representations to these students, whereas other students who are more verbal should get additional verbal explanations. Yet, according to dual coding theory, we should give ALL students a relevant diagram *and* relevant verbal information to go along with it, and encourage the students to integrate the two.

Combining pictures with words can be helpful for all learners – not just those who like pictures.

If students are learning about the anatomy of an animal cell, giving them a diagram with no words on it at all will not likely help them with the anatomy (though there is an exception, which we will get to in the next paragraph). But, giving them a diagram that is labeled and explains how the different components of the cell work together is much more likely to be beneficial.

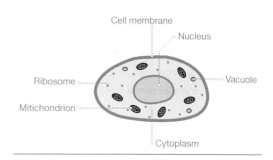

Cell membrane
Nucleus
Ribosome
Vacuole
Mitichondrion
Cytoplasm

Examples of an unlabeled and labeled diagram

There is one exception we can think of where an unlabeled diagram might actually be more helpful. If the students already understand how the different aspects of the animal cell work together, they could use the unlabeled diagram to practice retrieval of the various pieces, and how they all work together. In this case, the students would be combining dual coding (visual information with verbal information), elaborative interrogation (describing and explaining how things work), and retrieval practice (bringing information to mind, see Chapter 10).

DUAL CODING CAVEATS

The idea of dual coding often appears as multimedia learning, because here the material is represented in multiple forms (Meyer & Anderson, 1992). However, as with most things in life, there's always a risk of "too much of a good thing." One problem is that sometimes, the visuals we choose might not be all that relevant to the content being studied. In these cases, visuals may do nothing to help learning, and even worse, might actually hurt learning by producing irrelevant but appealing distractions known in the literature as "seductive details" (Harp & Mayer, 1997).

Another problem is that sometimes combining too many words and visuals can actually hurt learning. Too much information at once can lead to cognitive overload (see Chapter 6), where "the learner's intended cognitive processing exceeds the learner's available cognitive capacity" (Mayer & Moreno, 2003, p. 43). If the demands of a learning activity require too much cognitive capacity, then students will not fully benefit from the activity.

Thus, presenting information to students as words and visuals can help them learn, and learn in a meaningful way. However, if a student experiences cognitive overload trying to process all of the information in a meaningful way, then dual coding can harm learning. For example, the placing of labels in a diagram is important. That is, if labels are not placed conveniently near the aspects that are being labeled, this can create undesirable cognitive load and potentially impede learning (Mayer & Moreno, 2003) (see over).

But, cognitive overload is not specifically a problem with dual coding; cognitive overload can be an obstacle in almost all learning situations. Just because dual coding *can* lead to cognitive overload doesn't mean it *has* to. For some general suggestions about how to

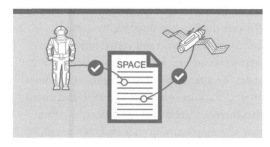

Any pictures accompanying written material must be relevant to target concepts.

reduce cognitive load when using dual coding learning strategies, see Chapter 11: Tips for teachers.

CHAPTER SUMMARY

Understanding can be developed through a process called elaboration, which involves connecting new information to pre-existing knowledge and describing things in many details. In practice, elaboration could mean many different things, but the common thread is that elaboration involves adding features to existing memories. In this chapter, we discuss three specific techniques that can be used to encourage elaboration. (1) Elaborative interrogation involves students asking "how" and "why" questions about the concepts they are studying, and then trying to answer these questions. (2) Concrete examples can provide several advantages to the learning process: (a) they can concisely convey information, (b) they can provide students with more concrete information that is easier to remember, and (c) they can take advantage of the superior memorability of pictures relative to words. Finally, (3) dual coding theory suggests that providing both verbal and pictorial representations of the same information enhances learning and memory. Given that pictures are generally remembered better than words, it is important to ensure that the pictures students are provided with are helpful and relevant to the content they are expected to learn.

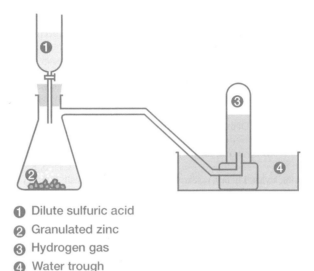

① Dilute sulfuric acid
② Granulated zinc
③ Hydrogen gas
④ Water trough

Labels are placed far away from the aspects being labeled

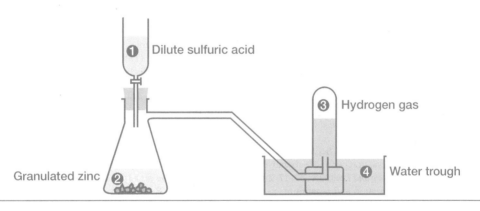

① Dilute sulfuric acid

③ Hydrogen gas

Granulated zinc ②

④ Water trough

Labels are placed near the aspects being labeled

REFERENCES

Anderson, J. R. (1983). A spreading activation theory of memory. *Journal of Verbal Learning and Verbal Behavior, 22*, 261–295.

Bauernschmidt, A. (2017, May). Two examples are better than one [Blog post]. *The Learning Scientists Blog*. Retrieved from www.learningscientists.org/blog/2017/5/30-1

Bellezza, F. S., Cheesman, F. L., & Reddy, B. G. (1977). Organization and semantic elaboration in free recall. *Journal of Experimental Psychology: Human Learning and Memory, 3*, 539–550. doi:10.1037/0278-7393.3.5.539

Carbonneau, K., Marley, S. C., & Selig, J. P. (2013). A meta-analysis of the efficacy of teaching mathematics with concrete manipulatives. *Journal of Educational Psychology, 105*, 380–400.

Chi, M. T., Feltovich, P. J., & Glaser, R. (1981). Categorization and representation of physics problems by experts and novices. *Cognitive Science, 5*, 121–152.

Chi, M. T., de Leeuw, N., Chiu, M. H., & LaVancher, C. (1994). Eliciting self-explanations improves understanding. *Cognitive Science, 18*, 439–477.

Chi, M. T., Bassok, M., Lewis, M. W., Reimann, P., & Glaser, R. (1989). Self-explanations: How students study and use examples in learning to solve problems. *Cognitive Science, 13*, 145–182.

Clinton, V., Alibali, M. W., & Nathan, M. J. (2016). Learning about posterior probability: Do diagrams and elaborative interrogation help? *The Journal of Experimental Education, 84*, 579–599.

Craik, F. I., & Lockhart, R. S. (1972). Levels of processing: A framework for memory research. *Journal of Verbal Learning and Verbal Behavior, 11*, 671–684.

Craik, F. I., & Tulving, E. (1975). Depth of processing and the retention of words in episodic memory. *Journal of Experimental Psychology: General, 104*, 268–294.

Dunn, R. (2000). Learning styles: Theory, research, and practice. *National Forum of Applied Educational Research Journal, 13*, 3–22.

Gick, M. L., & Holyoak, K. J. (1980). Analogical problem solving. *Cognitive Psychology, 12*, 306–355.

Gick, M. L., & Holyoak, K. J. (1983). Schema induction and analogical transfer. *Cognitive Psychology, 15*, 1–38.

Harp, S. F., & Mayer, R. E. (1997). The role of interest in learning from scientific text and illustrations: On the distinction between emotional interest and cognitive interest. *Journal of Educational Psychology, 89*, 92–102.

Hirshman, E. (2001). Elaboration in memory. In N. J. Smelser & P. B. Baltes (Eds.), *International encyclopedia of the social and behavioral sciences* (pp. 4369–4374). Oxford: Pergamon.

Kahl, B., & Woloshyn, V. E. (1994). Using elaborative interrogation to facilitate acquisition of factual information in cooperative learning settings: One good strategy deserves another. *Applied Cognitive Psychology, 8*, 465–478.

Karpicke, J. D., & Smith, M. A. (2012). Separate mnemonic effects of retrieval practice and elaborative encoding. *Journal of Memory and Language, 67*, 17–29.

Mandler, G. (1979). Organization and repetition: Organizational principles with special reference to rote learning. In L. G. Nillson (Ed.), *Perspectives on memory research* (pp. 293–327). Hillsdale, NJ: Lawrence Erlbaum Associates.

Mayer, R. E., & Moreno, R. (2003). Nine ways to reduce cognitive load in multimedia learning. *Educational Psychologist, 38*, 43–52.

McDaniel, M. A., & Donnelly, C. M. (1996). Learning with analogy and elaborative interrogation. *Journal of Educational Psychology, 88*, 508–519.

McNeil, N. M., Uttal, D. H., Jarvin, L., & Sternberg, R. J. (2009). Should you show me the money? Concrete objects both hurt and help performance on mathematics problems. *Learning and Instruction, 19*, 171–184.

Meyer, R. E., & Anderson, R. B. (1992). The instructive animation: Helping students build connections between words and pictures in multimedia learning. *Journal of Educational Psychology, 4*, 444–452.

Nestojko, J. F., Bui, D. C., Kornell, N., & Bjork, E. L. (2014). Expecting to teach enhances learning and organization of knowledge in free recall of text passages. *Memory & Cognition, 42*, 1038–1048.

Paivio, A. (1971). *Imagery and verbal processes.* New York: Holt, Rinehart and Winston.

Paivio, A. (1986). *Mental representations: A dual coding approach.* New York: Oxford University Press.

Paivio, A., & Csapo, K. (1969). Concrete image and verbal memory codes. *Journal of Experimental Psychology, 80*, 279–285.

Paivio, A., & Csapo, K. (1973). Picture superiority in free recall: Imagery or dual coding? *Cognitive Psychology, 5*, 176–206.

Paivio, A., Walsh, M., & Bons, T. (1994). Concreteness effects on memory: When and why? *Journal of Experimental Psychology: Learning, Memory, and Cognition, 20*, 1196–1204.

Pashler, H., McDaniel, M., Rohrer, D., & Bjork, R. (2008). Learning styles concepts and evidence. *Psychological Science in the Public Interest, 9*, 105–119.

Postman, L. (1976). Methodology of human learning. In W. K. Estes (Ed.), *Handbook of learning and cognitive processes: Volume 3, Approaches to human learning and motivation* (pp. 11–69). Hillsdale, NJ: Lawrence Erlbaum Associates.

Pressley, M., McDaniel, M. A., Turnure, J. E., Wood, E., & Ahmad, M. (1987). Generation and precision of elaboration: Effects on intentional and incidental learning. *Journal of Experimental Psychology: Learning, Memory, and Cognition, 13*, 291–300.

Smith, B. L., Holliday, W. G., & Austin, H. W. (2010). Students' comprehension of science textbooks using a question-based reading strategy. *Journal of Research in Science Teaching, 47*, 363–379.

Smith, M. A. (2014). *The process of elaboration and implications for retrieval processes* (Doctoral dissertation). Retrieved from ProQuest Dissertations and Theses database. (UMI No. 3669553).

Smith. M. (2016, October). What do students remember from our examples? [Blog post]. *The Learning Scientists Blog.* Retrieved from: www.learningscientists.org/blog/2016/10/20-1

Tajika, H., Nakatsu, N., Nozaki, H., Neumann, E., & Maruno, S. (2007). Effects of self-explanation as a metacognitive strategy for solving mathematical word problems. *Japanese Psychological Research, 49*, 222–233.

Woloshyn, V. E., & Stockley, D. B. (1995). Helping students acquire belief-inconsistent and belief-consistent science facts: Comparisons between individual and dyad study using elaborative interrogation self-selected study and repetitious-reading. *Applied Cognitive Psychology, 9*, 75–89.

Woloshyn, V. E., Pressley, M., & Schneider, W. (1992). Elaborative-interrogation and prior-knowledge effects on learning of facts. *Journal of Educational Psychology, 8*, 115–123.

The act of retrieval itself is thought to strengthen memory, making information more retrievable later.

Retrieval practice gives students feedback on what they know and do not know, and gives teachers feedback too.

What makes retrieval practice such a valuable strategy is that it helps promote meaningful learning.

If the goal is long–lasting, durable learning, then retrieval practice is a highly effective learning strategy.

Retrieval practice doesn't have to be done with a formal test.

Teachers can promote retrieval practice in the classroom by giving frequent low- or no–stakes quizzes.

Any retrieval practice format that teachers can implement in their classrooms is likely to benefit students.

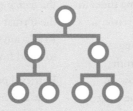

Scaffolding by giving hints and guides is a great way to help increase retrieval success.

Retrieval practice can feel difficult, but it's important not to fall into the trap of feel-good learning.

REINFORCEMENT OF LEARNING

Retrieval practice

Every time a memory is brought to mind, it is reconstructed and reinforced. When students take a quiz, they're not just checking their memory – they are enhancing it.

The act of retrieval itself is thought to strengthen memory, making information more retrievable later.

RETRIEVAL PRACTICE: WHAT'S THE MAIN IDEA?

In the evenings when I (Megan) have returned from work and my husband and I are cooking dinner, we exchange stories from our day. I tell my husband how a particular lesson went in class, or about a really fun meeting I had with a student about a new research project. My husband tells me about having lunch with his coworkers and bugs in a system that he had to work to fix. I imagine many of those reading this book do something similar with their families, roommates, or even on the phone with those who are not living near them. When we do this, we are thinking back to the events of our day and bringing them to mind. In other words, we are practicing retrieval.

Retrieval practice involves reconstructing something you've learned in the past from memory, and thinking about it right now. In other words, a while after learning something by reading or hearing about it, if you bring the information to mind then you are practicing retrieval. Retrieval practice improves learning compared to re-reading the information (Roediger & Karpicke, 2006), and even compared to other strategies that are thought by many to help learning, such as making a concept map with the written material you're studying right in front of you (Karpicke & Blunt, 2011).

Bringing information to mind can happen during several different scenarios, but the most common is when students are taking tests or quizzes: when answering a question on a test or quiz, students are required to bring information to mind. Because of this, the learning benefits from retrieval practice have been referred to as the *testing effect* (Duchastel, 1979). However, the format of retrieval doesn't have to be a test. Really, anything that involves brining information to mind from memory improves learning.

Retrieval practice as a learning strategy is not new. The first paper about retrieval practice was published in 1909 (Abbott, 1909) – over 100 years ago. In 1989, Glover wrote a paper titled *The Testing Phenomenon: Not Gone but Nearly Forgotten*. So, even in the late 1980s researchers were writing about "old" strategies and were surprised that they weren't being picked up broadly in practice.

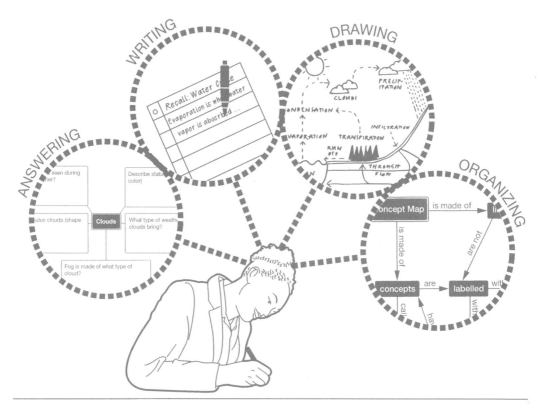

There are many ways to practice retrieval.

HOW DOES RETRIEVAL BENEFIT LEARNING?

Retrieval practice benefits learning in many different ways (Roediger, Putnam, & Smith, 2011). Quite possibly the most surprising finding is that retrieval practice has a direct effect on learning (Smith, Roediger, & Karpicke, 2013). This means that when we bring information to mind from memory, we are changing that memory, and research suggests we are making the memory both more durable and more flexible for future use.

This happens even in the absence of feedback or restudy opportunities (the fact that practicing retrieval helps students learn what they know and don't know is an indirect benefit of retrieval practice, which we will cover shortly). The

The question of concern here is not so much whether tests enhance memory—the data overwhelmingly indicate they do. Instead, the emphasis is on why a test given between an initial learning episode and a final test enhances students' memory performance.
(1989, p. 392)

John Glover

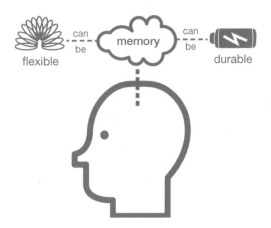

Knowing what students know and don't know can help educators allocate classroom time appropriately, or can help students allocate independent study time appropriately. Some research even finds that retrieval practice can also make restudy opportunities even more effective. In other words, if students practice retrieval prior to looking over their course materials, they will learn more from looking over the course materials than they would have if they hadn't practice retrieval beforehand (Izawa, 1966; McDermott & Arnold, 2013). This is called *test-potentiated learning,* and while the effects are not always robust, this potential benefit to retrieval practice is likely to add value to an already valuable learning strategy.

mechanisms underlying the benefits of retrieval practice are not fully understood yet, and much research is currently focused on understanding them (e.g., Carpenter, 2011; Lehman, Smith, & Karpicke, 2014), but for practical purposes simply knowing there is a direct benefit of retrieval practice for learning is useful!

In addition to direct benefits, retrieval practice can also benefit learning indirectly. What this means is that retrieval practice produces something else, and that something else improves learning. For example, retrieval practice gives students feedback on what they know and do not know, and gives teachers feedback about the students' understanding of the material.

WHAT TYPES OF INFORMATION CAN RETRIEVAL PRACTICE BE USED WITH?

Practicing retrieval can help students memorize facts, and there are certainly times when students need to memorize information. But retrieval practice also helps the students use the information more flexibly in the future, applying what they know in new situations. What makes retrieval practice such a valuable strategy is that it helps promote meaningful learning, and is not just for memorization of facts.

For example, in one of Megan's studies (Smith, Blunt, Whiffen, & Karpicke, 2016), university students learned about the respiratory system by either practicing repeated retrieval – they read a passage and then typed what they could remember from the passage into the computer – or repeatedly reading the information.

One week later, the students took a short-answer test to assess learning. The assessment test included some questions that were taken verbatim from the passage, and these questions only required that the students remembered specific information that they read. However, other questions required the students to go beyond what they had read. For example, one

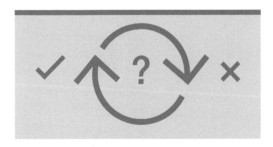

Retrieval practice gives students feedback on what they know and do not know, and gives teachers feedback too.

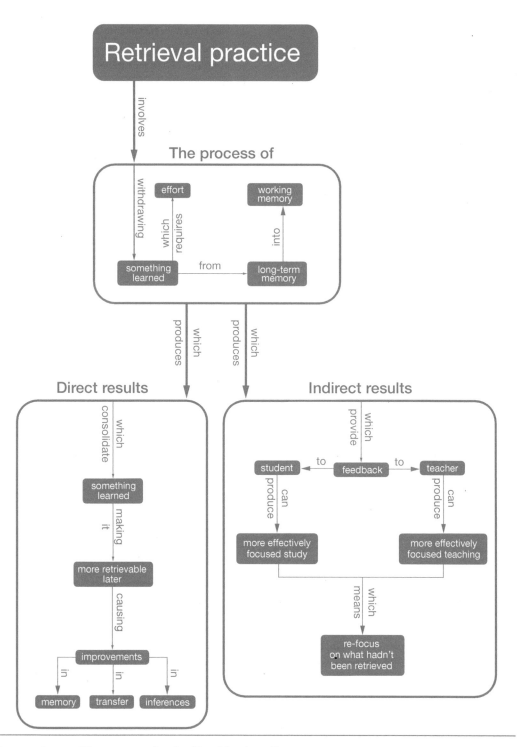

A concept map of the processes involved in retrieval practice.

What makes retrieval practice such a valuable strategy is that it helps promote meaningful learning.

question asked the students to imagine a disease, like polio, that paralyzes muscles. They were then asked to explain how this type of disease would affect the respiratory system.

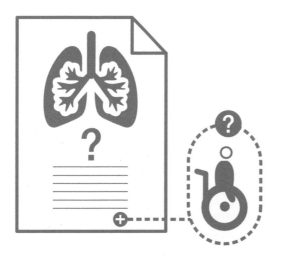

They had not read about polio or paralysis in the text, but they did learn about how muscles were used within the respiratory system. If they had understood the respiratory system, then they would be able to answer this novel question. The students were also asked about different types of environments, like ones with a lot of dust in the air. In the same experiment, students also read about how energy transfers from the sun. They were then asked to explain why it rarely rains in the desert where there are no large bodies of water.

Students were better able to answer these questions on the assessment after practicing retrieval than after repeatedly reading the passage. This is an example of retrieval practice helping students more flexibly use what they have learned via retrieval practice later.

WHEN DOES RETRIEVAL IMPROVE LEARNING?

Retrieval practice, like spaced practice, tends to produce learning benefits after a delay. If the assessment test is happening immediately, then students tend to perform best on the test after they have repeatedly read the information compared to when they have practiced retrieval. As was discussed in the spaced practice chapter: cramming works, but only in the short term. If the goal is longer-lasting, durable learning, then retrieval practice is a more effective learning strategy.

If the goal is long-lasting, durable learning, then retrieval practice is a highly effective learning strategy.

For example, in one study, students learned one passage about sea otters and another about the sun. Importantly, they learned the passages in two different ways. For one passage, students read two times. For the other, they read the passage and then practiced recall by writing as much as they could remember from that passage on a blank sheet of paper (Roediger & Karpicke, 2006, Experiment 1). Then, students either completed an assessment test five minutes, two days, or one week after learning. The assessment required them to, again, write out as much information from the passages as they could.

When the assessment occurred only five minutes after learning, the students remembered more from the passage that they read twice than the passage that they read and then practiced

GROUPS	TEXTS	STRATEGIES	RESULTS	TEST TIMINGS
A	Passage on sea otters	Reading ⊕ Re-reading	SUPERIOR SCORE ✓	5 minutes later
	Passage on the sun	Reading ⊕ Retrieval	INFERIOR SCORE ⊖	
B	Passage on the sun	Reading ⊕ Re-reading	INFERIOR SCORE ⊖	2 days later
	Passage on sea otters	Reading ⊕ Retrieval	SUPERIOR SCORE ✓	
C	Passage on sea otters	Reading ⊕ Re-reading	INFERIOR SCORE ⊖	1 week later
	Passage on the sun	Reading ⊕ Retrieval	SUPERIOR SCORE ✓	

The procedure in Roediger and Karpicke (2006, Experiment 1).

retrieval. However, after two days, and also after one week, the students remembered more from the passage that they learned by reading and practicing retrieval than the passage that they learned by reading twice.

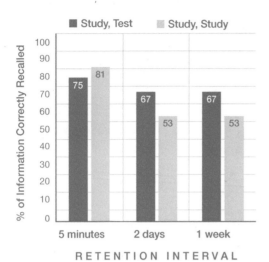

Results from Roediger and Karpicke (2006, Experiment 1).

RETRIEVAL PRACTICE: WHAT COUNTS?

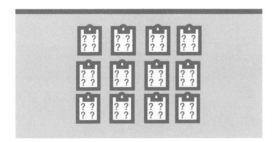

Retrieval practice doesn't have to be done with a formal test.

Retrieval-based learning activities are anything that require students to bring information to mind: students can write out everything they know on a blank sheet of paper (Roediger & Karpicke, 2006), create concept maps from memory (Blunt & Karpicke, 2014), draw a

diagram from memory (Nunes, Smith, & Karpicke, 2014), or even explain what they can remember to a peer, teacher, or parent (Putnam & Roediger, 2013).

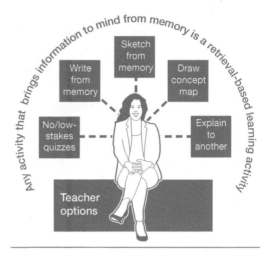

Any activity that requires students to bring information to mind from memory is a retrieval-based learning activity.

Below we discuss specific retrieval practice strategies that have been used in the classroom, as well as some caveats to bear in mind.

FREQUENT LOW-STAKES QUIZZES

Teachers can promote retrieval practice in the classroom by giving frequent low- or no-stakes quizzes.

Research on the benefits of test-taking suggests that when pressure to perform well on a test is increased, the learning benefits from retrieval

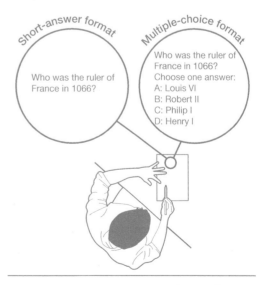

during the tests can decrease (Hinze & Rapp, 2014). However, this does not mean teachers should shy away from giving tests! Research also shows that frequent quizzing in the classroom can actually reduce overall test anxiety (Smith, Floerke, & Thomas, 2016). Together, this means if teachers can give frequent tests or quizzes that are worth smaller numbers of points, or no points at all, then the pressure to perform well will be reduced and this can help alleviate test anxiety when the students do take the higher-stakes tests or exams.

We feel that giving frequent quizzes is important both to improve learning and to help students get used to answering questions, even though many students may not like tests or quizzes. At some point in the child's life, they are going to have to take a test of some sort, and in fact they are probably going to need to take a number of high-stakes tests throughout their education. These tests are unlikely to go away, and we are willing to wager that licensing exams and board exams for professionals are absolutely here to stay (and, would you really want to be treated by a doctor who had failed their boards?) So, why not teach students the value of testing, and help them alleviate the parts of the tests they don't like?

We think this can be illustrated well with an analogy. Imagine you have a child who does not like to eat vegetables. We know that kids (and adults) should eat vegetables to get proper nutrition. One solution to try to help your child get their vegetables might be to puree the vegetables and hide them in a dessert, such as brownies, especially if the child is allowed dessert here and there anyway. This can be a great way to help increase vegetable intake, but I think most parents would agree that vegetables shouldn't *only* be hidden in the dessert. Kids need to learn to eat their vegetables so that it becomes part of their regular routine.

We think about tests and quizzes in the same way. It's fine, even desirable to "hide" retrieval

in other fun activities aside from taking tests. However, teaching students to take tests and making this part of their routine can help build good learning habits for the future, and can make those big standardized tests less scary when students are required to take them.

DOES TEST FORMAT MATTER?

One natural question that often comes up is what format should the quiz questions be? The two most common formats are short-answer and multiple-choice formats. Short-answer questions require the student to think of and produce the answer, while multiple-choice questions provide several alternatives (usually three to five) and require that the student select the one best answer to the question.

There has been some research showing that short-answer questions might improve learning more than multiple-choice questions because they require students to produce the answer (Kang, McDermott, & Roediger, 2007). Yet often multiple-choice questions are easier to administer and to grade, and we know this is very important for teachers who are busy. So, what is the solution?

Short-answer vs. multiple choice question formats.

One solution might be to combine the two formats to create a hybrid format. If teachers are able to administer quizzes on the computer, this is a viable option (Park, 2005). In a hybrid format, students would first answer a question in short-answer format and then go to the next screen to select among multiple alternatives.

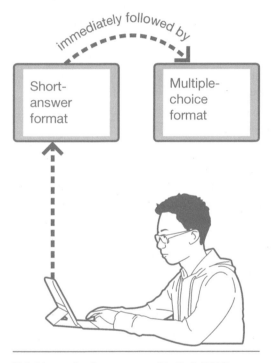

Hybrid question format as used in Park (2005).

In this way, teachers could allow the computer to grade the multiple-choice questions, and spot check the short-answer questions as they feel is necessary. This method would also have the benefit of giving students practice with multiple formats if these are test-taking skills the students need to learn. In absence of a computer to score multiple-choice questions, bubble sheets can work well for large classes or larger numbers of questions for quick scoring. And personally, we've

found that it is still faster to grade multiple-choice questions from paper and pencil tests than short-answer questions using paper and pencil.

However, worrying about the specific question format for quizzes may not be worth a teacher's time. Megan has conducted a series of experiments on this, and has found that learning differences between different retrieval practice formats tend to be small. In these experiments (Smith & Karpicke, 2014), students were randomly assigned to one of a few different conditions, and each group was given a different retrieval-practice format. Some students answered multiple-choice questions, some answered short-answer questions, and others answered hybrid questions. Finally, some students were in a control group where they didn't answer questions at all. All the students read a text, took a quiz (except the control group), and then read statements containing the correct answer to all of the quiz questions. One week later, we gave the students an assessment test (see opposite).

On the assessment, students who practiced retrieval performed better than those in the control group, and the learning benefits of retrieval practice were quite large. However, differences between retrieval formats tended to be very small. There are a fair number of research papers that come to the same conclusion with university students (Williams, 1963), graduate students, (e.g., Clariana & Lee, 2001) and middle-school students (McDermott, Agarwal, D'Antonio, Roediger, & McDaniel, 2014).

The bottom line seems to be that retrieval practice is good, and so any retrieval practice format that teachers can smoothly implement in their classrooms is going to benefit students.

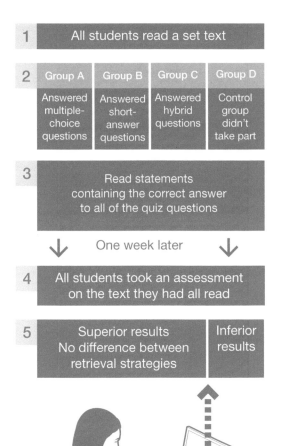

1	All students read a set text			
2	Group A	Group B	Group C	Group D
	Answered multiple-choice questions	Answered short-answer questions	Answered hybrid questions	Control group didn't take part
3	Read statements containing the correct answer to all of the quiz questions			

↓ One week later ↓

4	All students took an assessment on the text they had all read	
5	Superior results No difference between retrieval strategies	Inferior results

Procedure from Smith and Karpicke (2014).

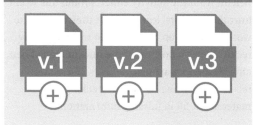

Any retrieval practice format that teachers can implement in their classrooms is likely to benefit students.

RETRIEVAL PRACTICE WITH YOUNGER CHILDREN OR DIFFICULT MATERIAL

While giving students a blank sheet of paper and asking them to recall is probably the easiest way to implement retrieval-based learning in the classroom, and has been shown to work over and over again with college students, it is not

always going to lead to improved learning. For example, Karpicke, Blunt, Smith, and Karpicke (2014) conducted an experiment with 4th grade students in their elementary classrooms.

Karpicke and his colleagues took 4th grade science textbooks from the schools and modified the materials to make them easier to read. Students first read the modified text, and then students were given a blank sheet of lined paper and instructed to write down as much as they could remember from the text. They were given plenty of time, but the 4th graders still had trouble remembering what they just read. The students only were able to write down 9 percent of the information on average. (Typically, in experiments with college students in which recall is effective at producing learning, the students are able to write down at least 50 percent of the material.) On a learning assessment four days later, the 4th graders did not perform any better after practicing recall compared to just reading the modified text. In other words, adding the extra recall task didn't improve learning.

The finding that recall did not improve learning, in this case, isn't actually surprising. If college students try to practice recall, but they don't recall much of anything, then they aren't likely to benefit from the activity either. Doing this won't hurt the students' learning, but they do need to work their way up to being able to successfully recall at least a portion of the information. Then, after recall, to maximize benefits researchers recommend going back and checking class materials to fill in missing information.

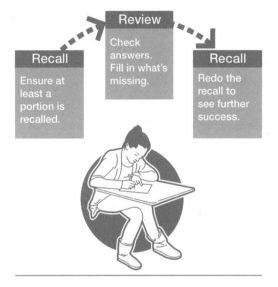

Recall, review, recall.

This is all well and good, but *what can we, as teachers, do to help facilitate successful retrieval?* This is particularly important for younger students who likely need more guidance and structure.

It seems that in order for retrieval practice to work well with students of any age, we need to make sure that students are successful. Scaffolding is a great way to help increase retrieval success. Scaffolding could be implemented with any student, but it may be particularly important with students who may struggle to recall on their own from the start.

In another experiment, Karpicke and colleagues tested ways of scaffolding retrieval with the 4th graders in their classrooms. To help guide the students to recall information, students were given partially completed concept maps – or

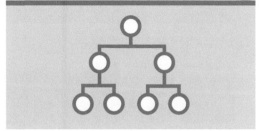

Scaffolding by giving hints and guides is a great way to help increase retrieval success.

diagrams that helps to represent relationships among ideas about a given topic. An example from the original research is shown below.

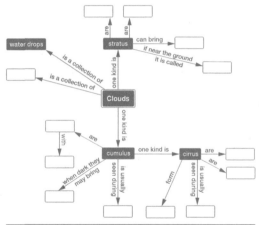

Sample partially completed concept map from Karpicke *et al.* (2014).

Students were first allowed to fill out the concept maps with the text in front of them. Then, the researchers took away the texts, and had the students complete these partially completed concept maps by recalling the information from memory. Using this scaffolded retrieval activity, the 4th grade students were much more successful on a learning assessment later, compared to what happened when they were just freely recalling. The next step was to see whether this general procedure would improve learning compared to a control group.

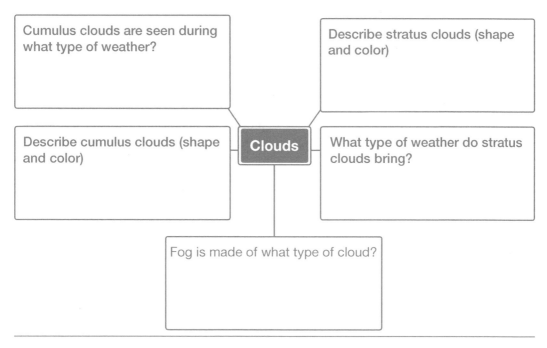

Sample blank concept map from Karpicke *et al*. (2014).

Knowing that scaffolding with concept maps helps students successfully retrieve information, the researchers completed one more experiment to compare the guided retrieval activity to a study-only control condition. Students completed a question map (shown below) with the text in front of them, and then completed another question map without the text. This was compared to a control group during which the students just read through the text twice.

On the learning assessment later, students remembered much more of the information when they used the map to practice retrieval compared to just reading. So, while practicing recall with a blank sheet of paper did not produce more learning than reading, practicing recall with helpful scaffolds in place did produce more learning than reading.

This example shows us that retrieval practice works well for students of many ages and abilities. But, for some students, writing out

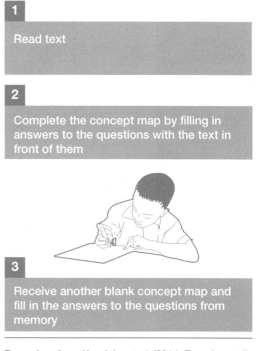

Procedure from Karpicke *et al*. (2014; Experiment 3).

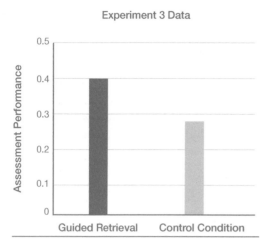

Experiment 3 Data

Results from Karpicke *et al*. (2014; Experiment 3).

everything they know on a blank sheet of paper may be a daunting task that does not lead to much successful retrieval. To increase success, teachers can implement scaffolded retrieval tasks, like the mapping activities presented here. With scaffolding, the students can successfully produce the information and work their way up to recalling the information on their own.

CHALLENGES IN USING RETRIEVAL PRACTICE

Balancing retrieval difficulty and success
One challenge to incorporating retrieval into the classroom is balancing difficulty of the retrieval activity and student success during

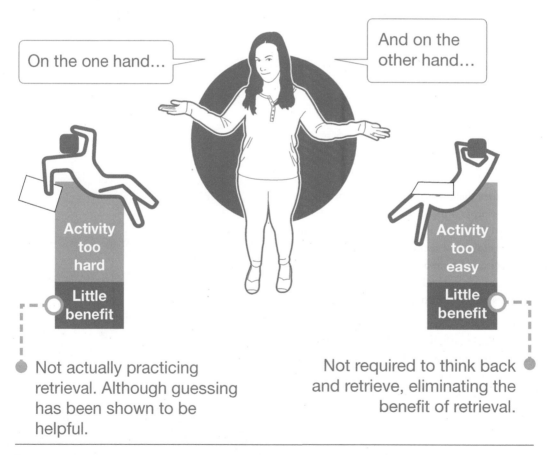

The key to optimizing a retrieval-based learning activity is to make sure that the students are being challenged to actually bring the information to mind from memory, but also that the students can be relatively successful at doing so.

the activity. The key to optimizing a retrieval-based learning activity is to make sure that the students are being challenged to actually bring the information to mind from memory, but also that the students can be relatively successful at doing so. Essentially, you want to have a healthy balance of difficulty and success.

On one hand, if the activity is too difficult and the students cannot produce any of the information, then they are not actually practicing retrieval and they are unlikely to benefit from the activity. There is some research suggesting that even a failed retrieval attempt can improve learning, and that producing a guess on a question where students have no chance of getting it right can also be helpful (Kornell, Hays, & Bjork, 2009; Potts & Shanks, 2014); however, teachers certainly do not want the students to fail at retrieval too often.

On the other hand, if the activity is too easy then the students may not be required to think back and retrieve, eliminating the benefit from retrieval. For example, I could ensure that students will be successful at retrieval by showing them three words at a time and then covering them up and asking the students to write those three words a few minutes later. Then I could show them the next three words in a book, cover them up and ask them to write those three words. If we went along in this way, the students would be able to "retrieve" entire books. But is this really making them think back and bring information to mind from their memories? Probably not. Thus, teachers will need to monitor the students' overall success while retrieving and try to adjust the difficulty of the activity accordingly (see Chapter 11, Tips for teachers, for more details).

CREATING GOOD MULTIPLE-CHOICE QUESTIONS

When they are well-constructed, multiple-choice questions can be just as good as

short-answer questions for retrieval practice (Little, Bjork, Bjork, & Angello, 2012). Teachers can increase the likelihood that they will improve learning by paying special attention to the way the alternatives are constructed. Multiple-choice questions work best to produce learning if the alternatives are plausible and require the students to retrieve the answer. Multiple-choice questions that only require that students pick the familiar answer are less likely to be helpful. That is, all the incorrect options on the test have to be at least *plausible* (see Butler, 2017).

Think of an extreme example. Imagine a teacher in history is asking students where the atomic bomb was dropped in Japan during World War II. If the alternatives were Hiroshima, New York City, Boston, and Philadelphia, then the students would not really need to retrieve information at all – they would be able to figure out by familiarity that Hiroshima is the answer because it is the only non-US city. However, if the alternatives were all plausible cities within Japan, then the student would probably have to think back and remember the name of the specific city in order to answer the question. Even more tricky is a question that includes correct answers to other questions as incorrect responses. For example, imagine you are asking students to retrieve the capital city of Lebanon in one question, and the capital city of Turkey in another. If you include both Beirut and Istanbul as possible answers to both questions, students can't just pick the most familiar answer on either question, as both should be equally familiar.

GIVING FEEDBACK

Another challenge to incorporating retrieval is providing feedback. As we already discussed, retrieval practice produces a direct effect on learning, and so feedback is not always necessary. However, feedback can make retrieval practice even more effective, and so we recommend giving feedback where possible. Giving feedback can be challenging because it may require extra work on the part of the teacher, and giving immediate feedback can be even more difficult when answers cannot immediately be scored.

However, despite the frequent mantra that feedback must be given instantly to be most effective (possibly stemming from the animal literature, where this is true! [Bouton, 2007]), research on the optimal timing of feedback is mixed. Some have found delaying the presentation of feedback to be most beneficial (Butler, Karpicke, & Roediger, 2007; Mullet, Butler, Berdin, von Borries, & Marsh, 2016), likely because this introduces spacing (see Chapter 8). Ultimately, it's best to give some feedback than none at all – and do not fret if you can't deliver it instantly.

The type of feedback that works best is also going to depend on the type of retrieval practice utilized. For example, one concern with using multiple-choice questions is that students may select the wrong answer thinking that it's true, and thus learn the wrong thing from the test. Research, however, has shown us that providing corrective feedback on multiple-choice tests is usually enough to combat these potentially negative effects (Butler & Roediger, 2008; Marsh, Roediger, Bjork, & Bjork, 2007).

Shying away from multiple-choice questions doesn't necessarily fix this problem. If students are answering short-answer questions, they may still produce (and consequently learn) the wrong information. In addition, research has shown that many college students are not very good at comparing a correct answer to a question to their own answer and determining what is correct and incorrect (Rawson & Dunlosky, 2007), so such misunderstandings may need to be addressed by the teacher.

ENCOURAGING STUDENTS TO USE RETRIEVAL PRACTICE

For those of us working with students who are transitioning to become more independent learners, another challenge is to encourage students to practice retrieval at home on their own. This challenge is not specific to retrieval practice; encouraging students to utilize any effective study strategy on their own can be difficult. Surveys of college students indicate that they do not often utilize the most effective study strategies, like practicing retrieval, and instead choose to use strategies that are less effective, like repeated reading (Hartwig & Dunlosky, 2012; Karpicke, Butler, & Roediger, 2009; Kornell & Bjork, 2007).

One big challenge to practicing retrieval for students is that intuitively retrieval practice can feel like it is not producing as much learning as we might want. For example, in one study that we described in Chapter 3, college students read a passage and then either read the passage three more times or practiced retrieval by writing everything they could remember on a blank sheet of paper three times (Roediger & Karpicke, 2006, Experiment 2). In the retrieval condition of this experiment, no feedback or restudy opportunities were given. Instead, the students wrote what they could remember on a blank sheet of paper, and then they were given a new blank sheet of paper and practiced retrieval again, and then finally a new blank sheet of paper to practice retrieval a third time. Then, the students were asked to predict how well they would perform on an exam in one week.

The students who read the passage four times were more confident in how well they would perform on the exam than those in the retrieval practice group. So, if we were to stop here, we might think that repeated reading is better than practicing retrieval. After all, the students who repeatedly read *think* they are going to do better on the upcoming test than the students who practiced retrieval.

However, on the test one week later, students who repeatedly read performed much worse than they predicted, while those who practiced retrieval actually do a little better than they thought they would. Importantly, the strategy that students thought would not be as good turned out to be best. Repeatedly reading the textbook or class notes in general tends to make students overconfident when predicting learning. Reading the information over and over makes the information seem more familiar, but this familiarity does not mean that students will be able to produce the information on a test, or apply what they have learned in new situations. In Chapter 12, we give tips for more independent students about how they can practice retrieval on their own, and warn them not to fall into the trap of "feel-good" learning strategies.

Retrieval practice can feel difficult, but it's important not to fall into the trap of feel-good learning.

CHAPTER SUMMARY

While tests are most often used for assessment purposes, a lesser known benefit of tests is that when students take tests they are practicing retrieval, which causes learning. The act of retrieval itself is thought to strengthen memory, making information more retrievable (easier to remember) later. In addition,

practicing retrieval has been shown to improve higher-order, meaningful learning, such as transferring information to new contexts or applying knowledge to new situations. Practicing retrieval is a powerful way to improve meaningful learning of information, and it is relatively easy to implement in the classroom.

REFERENCES

Abbott, E. E. (1909). On the analysis of the factors of recall in the learning process. *Psychological Monographs, 11*, 159–177.

Blunt, J. R., & Karpicke, J. D. (2014). Learning with retrieval-based concept mapping. *Journal of Educational Psychology, 106*, 849–858.

Bouton, M. E. (2007). *Learning and behavior: A contemporary synthesis.* Sunderland, MA: Sinauer Associates.

Butler, A. C. (2017, October). Multiple-choice testing: Are the best practices for assessment also good for learning? [Blog post]. *The Learning Scientists Blog.* Retrieved from www.learningscientists.org/blog/2017/10/10-1

Butler, A. C., & Roediger, H. L. (2008). Feedback enhances the positive effects and reduces the negative effects of multiple-choice testing. *Memory & Cognition, 36*, 604–616.

Butler, A. C., Karpicke, J. D., & Roediger, H. L. (2007). The effect of type and timing of feedback on learning from multiple-choice tests. *Journal of Experimental Psychology: Applied, 13*, 273–281.

Carpenter, S. K. (2011). Semantic information activated during retrieval contributes to later retention: Support for the mediator effectiveness hypothesis of the testing effect. *Journal of Experimental Psychology: Learning, Memory, & Cognition, 37*, 1547–1552.

Clariana, R. B., & Lee, D. (2001). The effects of recognition and recall study tasks with feedback in a computer-based vocabulary lesson. *Educational Technology Research & Development, 49*, 23–36.

Duchastel, P. C. (1979). Retention of prose materials: The effect of testing. *The Journal of Educational Research, 72*, 299–300.

Glover, J. A. (1989). The "testing" phenomenon: Not gone but nearly forgotten. *Journal of Educational Psychology, 81*, 392–399.

Hartwig, M. K., & Dunlosky, J. (2011). Study strategies of college students: Are self-testing and scheduling related to achievement? *Psychonomic Bulletin & Review, 19*, 126–134.

Hinze, S. R., & Rapp, D. N. (2014). Retrieval (sometimes) enhances learning: Performance pressure reduces the benefits of retrieval practice. *Applied Cognitive Psychology, 28*, 597–606.

Izawa, C. (1966). Reinforcement-test sequences in paired-associate learning. *Psychological Reports, 18,* 879–919.

Kang, S. H. K., McDermott, K. B., & Roediger, H. L. (2007). Test format and corrective feedback modulate the effect of testing on memory retention. *The European Journal of Cognitive Psychology, 19,* 528–558.

Karpicke, J. D., & Blunt, J. R. (2011). Retrieval practice produces more learning than elaborative studying with concept mapping. *Science, 331,* 772–775.

Karpicke, J. D., Butler, A. C., & Roediger, H. L. (2009). Metacognitive strategies in student learning: Do students practise retrieval when they study on their own? *Memory, 17,* 471–479.

Karpicke, J. D., Blunt, J. R., Smith, M. A., & Karpicke, S. S. (2014). Retrieval-based learning: The need for guided retrieval in elementary school children. *Journal of Applied Research in Memory and Cognition, 3,* 198–206.

Kornell, N., & Bjork, R. A. (2007). The promise and perils of self-regulated study. *Psychonomic Bulletin & Review, 14,* 219–224.

Kornell, N., Hays, J., & Bjork, R. A. (2009). Unsuccessful retrieval attempts enhance subsequent learning. *Journal of Experimental Psychology: Learning, Memory, and Cognition, 35,* 989–998.

Lehman, M., Smith, M. A., & Karpicke, J. D. (2014). Toward an episodic context account of retrieval-based learning: Dissociating retrieval practice and elaboration. *Journal of Experimental Psychology: Learning, Memory, and Cognition, 40,* 1787–1794.

Little, J. L., Bjork, E. L., Bjork, R. A., & Angello, G. (2012). Multiple-choice tests exonerated, at least of some charges: Fostering test-induced learning and avoiding test-induced forgetting. *Psychological Science, 23,* 1337–1344.

Marsh, E. J., Roediger, H. L., Bjork, R. A., & Bjork, E. L. (2007). The memorial consequences of multiple-choice testing. *Psychonomic Bulletin & Review, 14,* 194–199.

McDermott, K. B., & Arnold, K. M (2013). Test-potentiated learning: Distinguishing between direct and indirect effects of tests. *Journal of Experimental Psychology: Learning, Memory, and Cognition, 39,* 940–945.

McDermott, K. B., Agarwal, P. K., D'Antonio, L., Roediger, H. L., & McDaniel, M. A. (2014). Both multiple-choice and short-answer quizzes enhance later exam performance in middle and high school classes. *Journal of Experimental Psychology: Applied, 20,* 3–21.

Mullet, H. G., Butler, A. C., Berdin, B., von Borries, R., & Marsh, E. J. (2014). Delaying feedback promotes transfer of knowledge despite student preferences to receive feedback immediately. *Journal of Applied Research in Memory and Cognition, 3,* 222–229.

Nunes, L., Smith, M. A., & Karpicke, J. D. (2014, November). *Matching learning styles and retrieval activities.* Poster presented at the 55th Annual Meeting of the Psychonomic Society, Long Beach, CA.

Park, J. (2005). Learning in a new computerised testing system. *Journal of Educational Psychology, 97,* 436–443.

Potts, R., & Shanks, D. R. (2014). The benefit of generating errors during learning. *Journal of Experimental Psychology: General, 143,* 644–667.

Putnam, A. L., & Roediger, H. L. (2013). Does response mode affect amount recalled or the magnitude of the testing effect? *Memory & Cognition, 41,* 36–48.

Rawson, K. A., & Dunlosky, J. (2007). Improving students' self-evaluation of learning for key concepts in textbook materials. *European Journal of Cognitive Psychology, 19,* 559–579.

Roediger, H. L., & Karpicke, J. D. (2006). Test-enhanced learning: Taking memory tests improves long-term retention. *Psychological Science, 17,* 249–255.

Roediger, H. L., Putnam, A. L., & Smith, M. A. (2011). Ten benefits of testing and their applications to educational practice. In J. Mestre & B. Ross (Eds.), *Psychology of learning and motivation: Cognition in education* (pp. 1–36). Oxford: Elsevier.

Smith, A. M., Floerke, V. A., & Thomas, A. K. (2016). Retrieval practice protects memory against acute stress. *Science, 354*(6315), 1046–1048.

Smith, M. A., & Karpicke, J. D. (2014). Retrieval practice with short-answer, multiple-choice, and hybrid formats. *Memory, 22,* 784–802.

Smith, M. A., Roediger, H. L., III, & Karpicke, J. D. (2013). Covert retrieval practice benefits retention as much as overt retrieval practice. *Journal of Experimental Psychology: Learning, Memory and Cognition, 39,* 1712–1725.

Smith, M. A., Blunt, J. R., Whiffen, J. W., & Karpicke, J. D. (2016). Does providing prompts during retrieval practice improve learning? *Applied Cognitive Psychology, 30,* 544–553.

Williams, J. P. (1963). Comparison of several response modes in a review program. *Journal of Educational Psychology, 54,* 253–360.

Part 4

TIPS FOR TEACHERS, STUDENTS,
AND PARENTS

TIPS FOR TEACHERS

SPACING	ELABORATION	CONCRETE EX	VISUALS	RETRIEVAL

SPACING

Teachers can introduce these spacing techniques to their students in two ways:

1 By creating opportunities to revisit information throughout the semester (spacing), or within one lesson (interleaving)

2 By helping students to create their own effective study schedules.

ELABORATION

To encourage elaboration, help students to come up with relevant "how" and "why" questions, about what they are studying.

Then, help students come up with answers to these questions, and verify their accuracy in their study materials. Providing students with feedback on the relevance and depth of their questions can help them learn to use this technique more independently.

CONCRETE EX

When you present an abstract concept, use more than one concrete example to explain the idea.

Preferably, your examples will differ in terms of surface details, to help students generalize from the example to the idea.

VISUALS

Have students compare pictures in their textbooks to the related text. How are they similar. How are they different?

Then, have students attempt to describe a picture with words, and/or draw a visual representation of what they are reading in the text.

RETRIEVAL

You can insert retrieval practice into any number of activities.

The key is to ensure that students are bringing information to mind. You can promote retrieval practice in the classroom by giving frequent low- or no-stakes quizzes.

By providing frequent quizzes, you ensure that the overall stake of each individual quiz naturally becomes lower.

TIPS FOR TEACHERS

The six strategies backed by cognitive psychological research can all be implemented in the classroom by teachers who want to improve their students' learning. Now that we have described strategies related to planning, development, and reinforcement, we discuss practical ways that teachers can implement these strategies in their classrooms.

PLANNING (SPACING)

Teachers can introduce spaced practice techniques to their students in two ways: (1) by creating opportunities to revisit information throughout the semester (spacing) or within one lesson (interleaving); and (2) by helping students to create their own effective study schedules.

HOW TO IMPLEMENT SPACED PRACTICE IN THE CLASSROOM

How you implement spaced practice in the classroom is going to depend on a lot of things: your particular subject, your students' ages and levels of understanding, the amount of time you have to plan, and the flexibility of your curriculum. The types of changes you can make range from completely overhauling your curriculum in order to spiral all topics throughout the year, to simply implementing spaced homework assignments. In general, we recommend the latter, because small changes you make in your teaching with large impacts are always going to be more welcome compared with large changes that have the potential to create change but are costly and could also introduce new problems (see the book *Small Teaching* by

James Lang [2016] for many examples of such small changes). With this in mind, here are some ideas to try:

- Give lagged homework, so that students have to do homework on a topic you taught a while back.
- Integrate brief reviews of previous ideas into later classes (Benney, 2016).
- Give students opportunities to engage with material covered in previous classes – this can be most effectively done with spaced quizzes.

HOW TO GET STUDENTS TO SPACE OUT THEIR STUDYING

Getting students to use spaced practice is really hard. Think back to the last time that you had to plan for something well in advance, create a schedule, and stick to it. It might have been really difficult to stick to that schedule. This is very difficult for everybody – it's not about students versus teachers, or kids versus adults. It seems that people in general just have a very hard time planning ahead, and then sticking to that plan; time management is a big issue. One way of getting students to plan out their studying is to have students work with their own schedules to create a realistic study plan. We have tried the following method with our students:

1. Have students complete a time log for a week or even two weeks where they record what they are doing every hour of every day of the week. We use a simple weekly schedule handout for this task. This gives the students a picture of how they are spending their time.
2. Once they have kept the log for at least a week, have the students reflect on where

there might be space for them to fit in some study sessions throughout the week.

3. Then, have the students take out their planners or calendars (or even, their favorite scheduling app), and ask them to block out specific times during the week when they can study specific topics – even just for a little bit.

4. Follow up with the students to check whether they are sticking to the schedule. Have them write down when they actually studied. How long are they spending? And how efficient are they – what are they actually doing while they are studying? Do they feel as though they are able to stay on task?

5. Have a class discussion about how the schedules are working out for everyone. By talking to one another, students will realize that they are not the only ones who are struggling to make spaced practice work with their schedules, and anecdotally we find that this can be reassuring.

6. Help students adjust their schedules. What worked? What didn't? What's the most efficient and realistic way of scheduling the study sessions for each student?

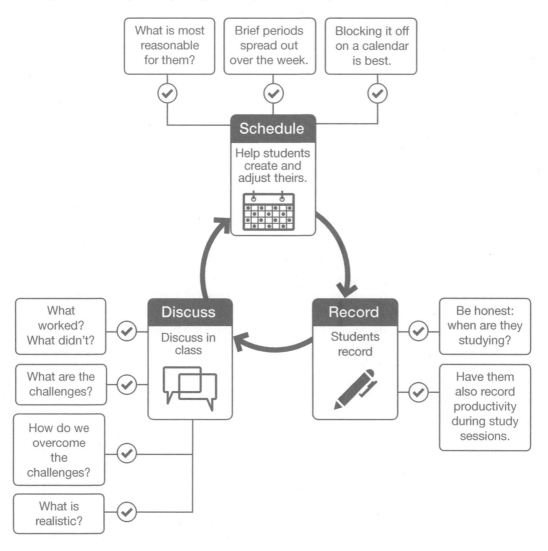

How much should students study every day? Well, if you think about the baseline – that students are typically not doing this at all until right before the exam – you'll see that every little bit helps. We were recently in England talking to students aged 14–15, and we asked them to get out their planners and make a commitment to study on three or four days in a given week, for as long as they thought was reasonable. We told the students: even if it's just five minutes, and that's the longest amount of time you could stick to, that's fine – because, guess what? Five minutes is infinitely longer than zero minutes. So just put five minutes into your planner, and see if you can stick to it. Most of our students tend to want to block off around 15 minutes or more at a time.

We should note that the fourth step in the planning activity above is really crucial. It's important to check in with the students and see whether they were able to stick to their plan, and what actually happened during each study session. So, for example, are they spending 20 minutes just re-reading their notes (see the next two chapters for why this may not be the most effective strategy)? Or are they spending 20 minutes engaged in an effective study strategy? Do they feel focused, or are they falling asleep?

Eventually, some patterns might emerge. They might realize that studying at midnight doesn't work so well, or studying in the afternoon is very difficult for them, but the ten minutes before getting on the bus works really well, or the ten minutes before football practice. This, of course, will vary depending on the individual and their other commitments. Often, our college students are burdened with all sorts of outside responsibilities: some are raising children, others are taking care of elderly relatives, and many are working full-time jobs concurrently with their studies. It's useless for the students just to put blocks of time into their schedules, but not

actually follow through – so it's important to adjust. Following up with students and seeing if their schedule works for them is very important, and gives students the opportunity to reflect and adjust their schedule to come up with one that is going to work for them in the long run.

One thing you could talk about to help students stick to a schedule is the practice of goal-setting and rewards. Many of us have a difficult time sticking to schedules that requires us to plan in advance, and having a strategy for how to mitigate procrastination and stick to the plan is always helpful. One particularly promising strategy for this is called the Wish Outcome Obstacle Plan (WOOP; Fallon, 2017). This strategy involves figuring out what it is you're wishing for and how it would feel to achieve this outcome (in this case, learning some information or doing well on a test); and then, crucially, coming up with a concrete plan for how to overcome internal obstacles that prevent you from sticking to your plan. I (Yana) have tried it out with students, having them use the WOOP strategy with a spaced practice study plan. What I found was that students have a really hard time coming up with *concrete* strategies for obstacle avoidance. They might write down an obstacle such as "I'll feel lazy," and a plan such as "I'll tell myself not to be lazy." You, as a teacher, can help students make that plan more concrete.

DEVELOPING UNDERSTANDING

Elaboration

- To encourage elaboration, help students to come up with relevant "how" and "why" questions about what they are studying. Then, help students come up with answers to these questions, and verify their accuracy in their study materials. Providing students with feedback on the relevance and depth of their questions can help them learn to use this technique more independently.

- You could also ask students questions that explicitly require them to compare and contrast different ideas within the same overall topic. Two questions that are great for comparing and contrasting are: "How are two ideas similar to one another?" and "How are these ideas different from one another?"
- Encourage students to make connections to their own memories or experiences, and compare ideas to learn how they are similar and different.
- Note that elaborative interrogation is best utilized by teachers to help develop understanding – not necessarily when first introducing a topic. Also, students may find this technique difficult and will benefit from deliberate practice of coming up with and answering relevant "how" and "why" questions.

Concrete examples

- When you present an abstract concept, use more than one concrete example to explain the idea. Preferably, your examples will differ in terms of surface details, to help students generalize from the example to the idea.
- To make sure the students understand how the concrete example applies to the abstract idea, help them to make the link between the various surface details and the underlying structure. This is the part students tend to find most difficult.
- Don't assume that students will know which part of the example is the most salient or relevant – make that explicit in your explanation.
- Use visual examples (i.e., examples illustrated with pictures) as well as verbal examples – see below for more on how to do this effectively.

Dual coding: How to use visuals effectively

- Have students compare pictures in their textbooks to the related text. How are they similar? How are they different?

- Then, have students attempt to describe a picture with words, and/or draw a visual representation of what they are reading in the text.
- Help students work their way up to drawing visuals from memory – that is, combining dual coding with retrieval practice (see Chapter 10).

The following recommendations for reducing cognitive load in multimedia learning are based on research reported by Mayer and Moreno (2003):

1. Slow down the presentation of words and pictures, and break these up into small segments. This way, the student is able to focus on smaller chunks of visual and verbal information at a time. Leaving small breaks in between the segments will help the students fully process the information from one segment before moving onto the next.

2. If segmenting isn't possible, providing pretraining about small components of a larger system before presenting the full verbal and visual description. For example, if a student is learning about how car brakes work, they might learn what each individual piece does during pretraining, then move on to learning how all of the components of the system work together using a diagram and a verbal description.

3. If you are presenting a diagram along with a verbal description, try presenting the words as narration. This way, students don't have to look at the diagram while trying to read the text.

4. Try presenting visuals and written words together so that students do not need to hold onto one representation while trying to process the other. If the words are spoken, narrate at the same time as the

visual is presented. In both cases, encourage the students to make connections between the visuals and the words.

5. Remove redundancies. For example, a teacher might present a diagram to students that includes text, and then also provide a verbal description. In this case, remove either the text or the verbal description so they are not processed at once. Presenting the words as spoken words and written words requires additional cognitive processing capacity.

6. When possible, reduce extraneous material (like background music or unnecessary animations). Removing aspects of the material or examples that are not essential to the material will help reduce cognitive load.

   Side note: This will work especially well when students are instructed to work with material (i.e., it is not an optional activity). If the activity is optional, reducing interesting aspects could reduce interaction. However, this is an empirical question!

7. Provide cues to the students to help them focus on the most important aspects of the learning activity. For example, telling the students before watching a video to pay attention to the explanation of why something works during the video clip.

Using some or all of these suggestions can help reduce the chance of cognitive overload while using dual coding. Note, these suggestions are not meant to be a precise recipe for how to construct dual coding learning opportunities, but rather guiding principles that can be used flexibly and considered, when appropriate. Some of these shouldn't be used at the same time, for example Tips 3 and 4. Tip 3 recommends narrating the words that are presented, while Tip 4 recommends putting words and visuals

together on the same page. But, if you do both of these, then you'll end up with both written and spoken words, which could lead to overload (see Tip 5). But, you could first use Tip 3 with one set of visuals, and then have the students work in small groups using Tip 4. You could even try a few of these at different times and space the presentations to further improve learning! Use your best judgment, and keep the concept of cognitive overload in mind when designing dual coding learning activities.

Reinforcement (retrieval practice)

How to implement retrieval practice in the classroom

You can insert retrieval practice into any number of activities; the key is to ensure that students are bringing information to mind.

- You can promote retrieval practice in the classroom by giving frequent low- or no-stakes quizzes. By providing frequent quizzes, you ensure that the overall stake of each individual quiz naturally becomes lower. In addition, you help students become accustomed to quizzes, which can reduce their anxiety in higher-stakes tests.
- Quizzes can be multiple-choice, or you can just ask students to write or sketch out what they can remember on a blank sheet of paper. The format of the quiz does not matter too much for learning. There are always going to be challenges that are specific to the type of format used (gradability, writing a good question, etc.). We recommend picking the format that works best for your class given the benefits and challenges.
- If you use multiple-choice questions, do make sure that all of the incorrect response options you provide are plausible and relevant, so that students can't guess the correct response by process of elimination or just by picking an answer that seems familiar.
- If you use short-answer questions, don't rely on students to accurately determine what

they got right or wrong. You may need to directly address misunderstandings produced on short-answer tests with the students rather than simply providing correct answers.

- You can also implement retrieval in the classroom in ways besides tests and quizzes as well. Retrieval-based learning activities are anything that require students to bring information to mind, and formal tests are not the only activity that does this!

- Have students write out everything they know on a blank sheet of paper, create concept maps from memory, draw a diagram from memory, or even explain what they can remember to a peer, teacher, or parent. Any activity that requires students to bring information to mind from memory is a retrieval-based learning activity.

- The method of retrieval you choose will depend on the students you are teaching and their familiarity with the content.

- Younger students, or students studying more difficult material, may need more guidance and structure to benefit from retrieval practice. In these cases, you can help students by scaffolding the retrieval task to help them achieve better performance during retrieval practice.

- Scaffolding could involve giving students a partially completed retrieval map, or other additional clues to help guide their retrieval process.

- Monitor students' success to make sure you have the difficulty of the retrieval practice task set to an appropriate level. If students are being required to recall too much information and are struggling, provide some hints or prompts to scaffold and help the students recall more. As the activity becomes too easy, then increase the difficulty by taking some of the supports away.

- Encourage students to practice retrieval on their own by giving them clear, concrete instructions for how to do it. However, this can be difficult for students to stick to, so do check in frequently to see if students are sticking to their intentions to practice retrieval!

FREQUENTLY ASKED QUESTIONS

How much space should I leave between teaching or quizzing the same information? What's the "optimal lag"?

While there's been lots of research into this question (Cepeda, Vul, Rohrer, Wixted, & Pashler, 2008), it becomes quite tricky to try to figure out the "optimal" amount of time between opportunities to revisit and/or retrieve information. In general, if opportunities to revisit are too close together, that's too much like cramming and won't be very effective. On the other hand, if they are too far apart, so much could be forgotten that it would be like re-learning information from scratch. Some apps programmed with complicated algorithms might be able to approximate optimal lag for a number of situations (Lindsey, Shroyer, Pashler, & Mozer, 2014). We also produced a beta version of a tool for teachers to help schedule review and retrieval opportunities. Teachers have also written about their experiences with trying to figure out the ideal lag (e.g., Benney, 2016; Tharby, 2014). However, our advice would be to keep it simple: give students more opportunities to review and retrieve the important information and material that needs to be remembered for longer.

In my class, I have students read before class, and then I give a lecture. Where should I place quiz questions for optimal learning – before or after the lecture?

It depends on your goals, and the overlap in content between the reading and the lecture. If there is total overlap between the two, then students will quickly figure this out and stop doing the reading, unless you quiz them on it before the lecture. If there is not total overlap, then a better solution would be to pull out some information that is only in the reading, and quiz them on that in addition to what's covered in the lecture. In that case, you can vary up the position of the quiz questions to maintain test expectancy throughout each class. In a recent paper, Yana investigated the placement of quiz questions throughout or at the end of a lecture (Weinstein, Nunes, & Karpicke, 2016); it didn't much matter for long-term learning.

Having some unexpected quizzes at the beginning of some lectures, and some at the end might be a good way to ensure that students arrive on time and stay for the whole class. If you can, consider including some quiz questions from previous lectures/readings in each class, to provide students with built-in opportunities for spaced practice!

If I ask ten questions about a topic, does that reinforce knowledge of the whole topic, or just the things I asked about?

Unfortunately, there is no straightforward answer to this question. It is a somewhat complex question that has to do with the notion of "transfer" of learned information to a new question or situation. While transfer is possible in some situations, it is quite hard to achieve. In fact, a study by Wooldridge, Bugg, McDaniel, and Liu (2014) tested a similar scenario to the one suggested in this question: they tested students on new information that they had not practiced, and found no improvement on that information relative to the ineffective study technique of highlighting. For the best chance of reinforcing knowledge of the whole topic, it does appear that retrieval practice on as much of the information as possible is preferable.

If testing helps learning correct information, then doesn't it also reinforce misconceptions when incorrect answers are retrieved?

Perhaps somewhat surprisingly, the answer is usually no: testing generally does not reinforce misconceptions – as long as there is feedback after the incorrect answer. Incorrectly retrieving

an answer and then receiving feedback is more beneficial than simply reading the correct answer without making a retrieval attempt. In one set of studies with vocabulary learning, students made guesses on items they had no idea about – their guesses had no basis whatsoever in any knowledge (Potts & Shanks, 2014). After these guesses, they then saw the correct response as feedback. At test, students were much more likely to identify the correct definitions of the studied words if they had previously made an incorrect guess and then seen the correct response, compared to just seeing the correct response without making a guess.

How does retrieval practice work with students at different ages or different abilities? Can elementary/primary students learn from retrieval practice?

Retrieving information seems to work well across the board. However, the way one approaches retrieval practice may need to be different depending on the students' abilities and background knowledge. If the students are unable to retrieve anything, then retrieval is unlikely to be very helpful. Some research has found that students around ten years old (4th grade) needed more guidance during retrieval compared to older students (Karpicke, Blunt, Smith, & Karpicke, 2014). For example, in that study, the ten-year-olds were unable to write out on a blank sheet of paper much of what they could remember from something they had just read. But, they were able to more successfully answer questions with the text in front of them and then move to answering the questions without the text. Maximizing benefits of retrieval practice seems to be about balancing the difficulty of the retrieval and the ability to successfully retrieve (Smith & Karpicke, 2014). Retrieval practice is hard, and the difficulty is helping to improve learning. However, if it is too difficult and students are unable to retrieve, then the opportunity won't be as beneficial as it might have been. Scaffolding retrieval opportunities for students who are new to a topic or struggling to produce what they read can improve the effectiveness of retrieval for these students. Try spacing out retrieval over time to help the students work their way up to better performance.

REFERENCES

Benney, D. (2016, October 16). (Trying to apply) spacing in a content heavy subject [Blog post]. Retrieved from https://mrbenney.wordpress.com/2016/10/16/trying-to-apply-spacing-in-science

Cepeda, N. J., Vul, E., Rohrer, D., Wixted, J. T., & Pashler, H. (2008). Spacing effects in learning a temporal ridgeline of optimal retention. *Psychological Science, 19*, 1095–1102.

Fallon, M. (2017). Guest Post: WOOP your way forward – a self-regulation strategy that could help you get ahead and stay ahead [Blog post]. *The Learning Scientists Blog.* Retrieved from www.learningscientists.org/blog/2017/7/4-1

Karpicke, J. D., Blunt, J. R., Smith, M. A., & Karpicke, S. S. (2014). Retrieval-based learning: The need for guided retrieval in elementary children. *Journal of Applied Research in Memory and Cognition, 3*, 198–206.

Lang, J. M. (2016). *Small teaching: Everyday lessons from the science of learning.* San Francisco: John Wiley & Sons.

Lindsey, R. V., Shroyer, J. D., Pashler, H., & Mozer, M. C. (2014). Improving students' long-term knowledge retention through personalized review. *Psychological Science, 25*, 639–647.

Mayer, R. E., & Moreno, R. (2003). Nine ways to reduce cognitive load in multimedia learning. *Educational Psychologist, 38*, 43–52.

Potts, R., & Shanks, D. R. (2014). The benefit of generating errors during learning. *Journal of Experimental Psychology: General, 143*, 644–667.

Smith, M. A., & Karpicke, J. D. (2014). Retrieval practice with short-answer, multiple-choice, and hybrid formats. *Memory, 22*, 784–802.

Tharby, A. (2014, June 12). Memory platforms [Blog post]. *Reflecting English Blog.* Retrieved from https://reflectingenglish.wordpress.com/2014/06/12/memory-platforms/

Weinstein, Y., Nunes, L. D., & Karpicke, J. D. (2016). On the placement of practice questions during study. *Journal of Experimental Psychology: Applied, 22*, 72–84.

Wooldridge, C., Bugg, J., McDaniel, M., & Liu, Y. (2014). The testing effect with authentic educational materials: A cautionary note. *Journal of Applied Research in Memory and Cognition, 3*, 214–221.

SPACING	ELABORATION	CONCRETE EX	VISUALS	RETRIEVAL

SPACING

Start planning early — the beginning of the semester, or even earlier. Set aside a bit of time every day, just for studying, even if your exams are months away.

Retrieval practice is difficult, and this difficulty is good.

Don't be fooled by strategies that make you feel like you're learning a lot.

ELABORATION

When you use elaborative interrogation, you ask yourself questions about how and why things work, and then produce the answers to these questions.

Make connections between multiple ideas to-be-learned.

CONCRETE EX

When you're studying, try to think about how you can turn ideas you're learning into concrete examples.

Making a link between the idea you're studying and a vivid, concrete example can help the lesson stick better.

VISUALS

When you have the same information in two formats — words and visuals — it gives you two ways to remember the information later on.

Combining these visuals with words is an effective way to study.

RETRIEVAL

You can use retrieval practice to improve learning during independent study.

The key is to make sure you bring information to mind after you've already learned something by reading it in a book or hearing it in class.

TIPS FOR STUDENTS

Students who are studying on their own can utilize planning, development, and reinforcement strategies to make their independent learning more effective. Here, we provide practical tips to help students apply effective learning strategies during their independent learning. Students can use these tips on their own, or teachers and parents could use this chapter to help guide students to create effective independent learning sessions.

PLANNING (SPACING)

Spaced practice is the exact opposite of cramming. When you cram, you study for a long, intense period of time close to an exam. When you space your learning, you take that same amount of study time and spread it out across a much longer period of time. Doing it this way, that same amount of study time will produce more long-lasting learning. For example, five hours spread out over two weeks is better than the same five hours right before the exam. But spacing your learning requires advance planning; you can't just decide to space out your studying at the last minute.

HOW TO STUDY WITH SPACED PRACTICE

- **Start planning early** – the beginning of the semester, or even earlier. Set aside a bit of time every day, just for studying, even if your exams are months away. This may seem strange at first if you are used to cramming right before an exam; but it's just a new habit that you will get used to if you persevere.

- **Review information from each class, but not immediately after class.** A good way to do this is to reserve some time one day after each of your classes meet. For example, if you have classes Monday, Wednesday, and Friday, you might review the information on Tuesday, Thursday, and Saturday respectively for each of those classes.

- **Spacing your learning doesn't mean you won't be studying at all right before the exam.** You can still study up until the exam – but instead of only studying then, spread it out so that you're studying days and weeks before the exam as well. You'll spend less time and learn more both in the short term and in the long term.

When you sit down to study, it's important that you don't just sit down and re-read your notes. Instead, you should use effective learning strategies such as those we describe in the rest of this chapter. After you study information from the most recent class, make sure to go back and study important older information to keep it fresh.

This may seem difficult and you may forget some information from day to day, but this is actually a good thing! You need to forget a little bit in order to benefit from spaced practice. Create small spaces (e.g., a few days) between your study sessions, and do **a little bit at a time** so that it adds up!

"BUT, BUT … CRAMMING WORKS!"

If you're reading this and you're skeptical because cramming has worked just fine for you in the past, here's why. Cramming can, indeed, do exactly what it suggests – cram some of the

Spacing: day 1

Spacing: day 2

Spacing: day 3

EXAM

Cramming: day 1

EXAM

information into your mind right before an exam. But, this isn't a good idea. It may not seem this way, but as students you do need to worry about long-term learning. You will need to remember information that you are learning now later on in your schooling. If you only worry about passing the one test now, you will have to work double as hard for the next test – even if it is just a few weeks later in the semester. The problem will continue to get worse and worse as you continue to advance through each semester. In other words, the cramming strategy that may work in the very short term, right now, will make things even more difficult for you later on, and "later" is closer than you may think.

There are at least three really big problems with cramming:

1. **First, cramming actually takes more time.** Think about it: if you learn more in the same amount of time spaced out (e.g., five hours in one-hour increments compared to one five-hour cram session), then you have to spend *more time during the cramming session* to get to the same level of learning.

2. **Second, as quickly as you learned that information, you will then also forget it.** You may do fine on the test, but all that extra time you spent during cramming? It will all have been wasted. If you had spaced your learning, you would forget much less after the test. No matter what you are learning – science, math, a foreign language – future learning will depend on previous learning. It is therefore very inefficient to forget everything you learned for one test, only to have to re-learn it again later along with new, more complicated information! This also applies to future classes, where it might be helpful to retain knowledge from a previous class.

3. **Another reason why cramming is a bad idea is that it inevitably replaces sleep,** which is very important for learning (Mazza *et al.*, 2016) and also for your mental and physical health more generally (Smith, Robinson, & Segal, 2016). So, resolve to form a healthy habit today and plan to space your learning!

Note: You need to get enough sleep

Sleep is extremely important for learning. Sleep deprivation can produce a number of physical health problems such as increasing weight gain and increasing chances for illness. Sleep deprivation can also cause impairments to attention, problem solving, and decision making (Smith, Robinson, & Segal, 2016). What is particularly important to realize is that even mild sleep deprivation can cause these effects. Some studies show that risk to health and cognitive impairments increases if you lose 1–2 hours of sleep each night! (In other words, if you're only getting about six hours of sleep per night, your cognitive functioning, including learning, is likely to suffer.) Further, research shows that getting sleep after learning improves performance later, especially for understanding information and problem solving (De Vivo *et al.*, 2017; Mazza *et al.*, 2016). This is another reason that cramming (as opposed to spacing) can be so bad for your learning. When you cram, you often lose sleep the night before the exam.

DEVELOPING UNDERSTANDING

Elaboration

Ask yourself questions about how and why things work, and then produce the answers to these questions. The specific questions that you ask yourself will depend, in part, on the topics you are studying (e.g., How does x work? Why does x happen? When did x happen? What caused x? What is the result of x? and so on). Here's how to do it:

- Start by **making a list** of all of the ideas you need to learn from your class materials. Then, go down the list and **ask yourself questions about how these ideas work and why**. As you ask yourself questions, go through your class materials (e.g., your text-book, class notes, any materials your teacher has provided, etc.) and look for the answers to your questions.

- As you continue to elaborate on the ideas you are learning, **make connections** between multiple ideas to be learned, and **explain how they work together**. A good way to do this is to take two ideas and **think about ways they are similar and ways they are different**.
- Describe how the ideas you are studying **apply to your own life experiences or memories**. In addition, as you go through your day, take notice of the things happening around you and **make connections** to the ideas you are learning in class. Doing this will engage an additional process that is highly effective: **spacing learning over time**.
- So far, we have suggested using elaborative interrogation as you study your class materials. At the start, you can definitely use your class materials to help you and fill in gaps as you elaborate. However, ideally, you should work your way up to describing and explaining the ideas you are learning on your own, without your class materials in front of you. In other words, you should **practice retrieval** of the information!

Concrete examples

- When you're studying, try to think about how you can turn ideas you're learning into concrete examples.
- Making a link between the idea you're studying and a vivid, concrete example can help the lesson stick better.
- Creating your own relevant examples will be the most helpful for learning; but before you get to that stage, if possible, always verify your examples with an expert.

Dual coding

When you have the same information in two formats – words and visuals – it gives you two ways of remembering the information later

on. Combining these visuals with words is an effective way to study.

- When you are looking over your class materials, find visuals that go along with the information and compare the visuals directly to the words.
- Cover up the text, and try to describe the visuals with words.
- Another time, you can do the opposite: read the text, and try to create your own visuals.
- This technique will be helpful regardless of whether you generally prefer pictures or words.
- Work your way up to practicing retrieval by drawing what you know from memory.

Reinforcement (retrieval practice)

You can use retrieval practice to improve learning during independent study. The key is to make sure you bring information to mind after you've already learned something by reading it in a book or hearing it in class. There are a lot of different ways to practice retrieval at home on your own. Here are some ideas:

- If your teacher provides **practice tests**, or there are **practice questions in your textbook**, make sure to attempt them – but without looking at your book or notes! Once you are done answering the questions, make sure to check your answers for accuracy. If there are questions that you got wrong, go back to those sections in the book or your class notes and review the material. If you're struggling to understand some of the ideas, go back to Chapter 10 and try using some of those strategies to strengthen your understanding.
- If you don't have practice questions (or you've already answered all of your practice questions a few times), **you can make your own questions**. This process takes a lot of

time, but if you create a study group you can each create a few questions and trade. Just make sure that the questions are about the content you are supposed to learn, and they aren't too easy. You want the questions to help you think back to the material you have learned and guide you to reconstruct the information. You also want to make sure to go beyond just remembering definitions of key terms. Definitions are important, but they are likely not the only thing you need to learn. Try creating broader questions, describing and explaining various topics, and even coming up with your own examples of the ideas.

- If you're having trouble coming up with specific questions, then you can **try just writing out everything you can remember on a blank sheet of paper**. If you have a lot of information to remember, try breaking it up into sections. You can use the headers in your textbook or general ideas provided by your teacher as prompts to help you recall as much as you can. When you are done, make sure to go back and review your class materials so that you can see what you missed and what you might need to work on more.

- You can also **create flashcards** to practice retrieval. The easiest way to create flashcards is to put a question or a prompt on one side of the card, and then put the answer on the other side. To use the flashcards to practice retrieval, look at the question side of the card and try to come up with the answer. Make sure that you are really retrieving the answer. Sometimes our students say they look at the question side and have a general idea that they know the answer, but this is not the same thing as really bringing the full answer to mind. You might even consider writing the answer down on a separate sheet of paper to really make sure you're bring-

ing it to mind. Then, after you've retrieved the answer yourself (or given it a good try) flip the card and take a look at the correct answer. There are also many apps for this if you prefer to use technology.

- Do make sure to practice retrieving more than just the simple concept definitions you write on your flashcards, though – try linking concepts, or trying to remember how two concepts are similar/different. A student of Yana's created her own method for using flashcards to get at more complex learning. She creates two stacks of cards – one with concepts, and the other with instructions for how to use the concepts to practice retrieval. For example, one instruction card could say "Pick two concept cards and describe how the two concepts are similar", whereas another might say "Pick one concept card and think of a real-life example related to it" (Adragna, 2016).

- If you like sketching, you can try to **draw everything you know about a topic from memory**! It doesn't have to be pretty – it just needs to make sense to you. As long as you're drawing what you know from memory, then you're practicing retrieval!

- While sketching, you can also try to **organize your ideas into a concept map**. A concept map is a way of showing how various concepts relate to one another. You create circles with ideas, and then create links between them that describe the relationship between the various ideas. The example opposite is a concept map about concept maps! Just make sure to always try to make the concept map from memory first!

Remember, retrieval practice can be difficult, whereas the alternative – reading and re-reading your notes and textbook – might feel easier. I (Megan) often tell my students: if your exam is going to be reading your textbook or notes as

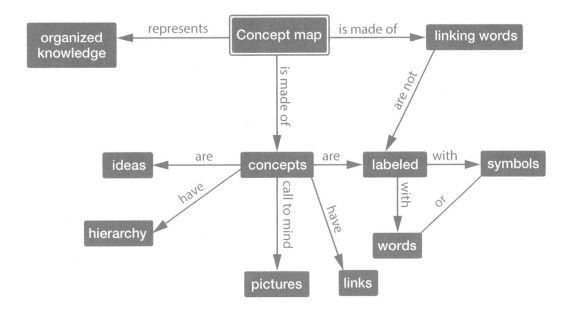

fast as you can without making any mistakes, then by all means repeatedly read to prepare for this exam. However, if the exam requires you to remember the information and apply it in new situations, then make sure you can actually do this during preparation! Practice retrieval, and you will learn the information in a more flexible and durable way.

Don't be fooled by strategies that make you feel like you're learning a lot. This is not necessarily the case! When you begin practicing retrieval, you probably will not be able to remember everything, and that's okay. It does not mean that you aren't learning anything from retrieval practice, or that retrieval practice is not "working for you." Retrieval practice is difficult, and this difficulty is good. Keep at it, and you can work your way up to being able to recall more.

FREQUENTLY ASKED QUESTIONS

How can I integrate the six study strategies into a study routine or regimen?

Spaced practice helps you figure out when you should study. Retrieval practice is the most important study strategy, and you should engage in this activity every time you study; it answers the overall question of how you should study. And finally: elaboration, concrete examples, and dual coding provide additional techniques that can be used in conjunction with retrieval practice. Good luck!

It sounds like there is a lot of overlap among the strategies. How do I know which is which? Should I try to use just one at a time?

Yes, there is definitely a lot of overlap among the strategies. This is not necessarily a bad thing! They are not meant to stand alone and can (and should) be used together. For example, spacing needs to be used with other strategies, because spacing is only about when to cover material, and not how to cover material. Retrieval practice can and should be integrated with all of the strategies. With elaboration, you can work your way up to being able to describe and explain how and why things work from memory. With dual coding, you can work your way up to being able to sketch out what you know from memory, and then describe those sketches in words from memory. By using dual coding with retrieval practice, you are encouraging multiple contexts and representations of the information AND retrieval of those representations, which both help learning! With concrete examples, you can work your way up to creating examples on your own from memory. If you have a fair amount of background knowledge about the topic you are studying, you may even be able to create your own concrete examples and trade them with your friends. Your friends could then describe and explain how the example fits the concept. Now we're combining retrieval, concrete examples, and elaborative interrogation into one group activity.

So, while the strategies can be used in isolation (aside from spacing, of course), they really can and should be used together. One thing to note, though, is that there is not a lot of literature directly testing the effectiveness of the combination of strategies compared to using them in isolation. There is a lot of evidence supporting the combination of spacing and retrieval practice, but not much with the combination of other strategies. But for the others, not as much research has been conducted … yet. Based on what we know, combining the strategies ought to be one of the best ways to maximize effective learning, and to keep students interested and engaged.

Does caffeine hurt or help learning?

There are lots of misunderstandings out there about nutrition and the brain, but the positive effects of caffeine you may have heard about aren't one of them. A recent meta-analysis suggests that coffee – in moderation, and particularly when you are fatigued – can increase the speed with which you react and your ability to persevere on a boring, repetitive task (McLellan, Caldwell, & Lieberman, 2016). In general, moderate levels of caffeine appear to help with attention. However, the research on caffeine's effects on memory is more mixed; there doesn't seem to be a consistent direct benefit of caffeine for memory. But to the extent that caffeine helps you stay on task while studying, it could be beneficial.

How can I take more effective notes in class?

Our answer to this question comes not from cognitive psychology, but from an adjacent field: applied behavior analysis. Research from this field recommends the use of "guided notes" to improve students' note-taking and learning from lectures (Barbetta & Skaruppa, 1995). The guided notes technique involves taking notes on a worksheet with cues and blank spaces so that you are prompted to take notes about specific concepts covered in the class. This method of note-taking has been shown to produce greater learning than other learning conditions such as presenting students with key points on PowerPoint slides, and/or having them take their own unstructured notes (Konrad, Joseph, & Eveleigh, 2009). If your teacher gives you guided notes, then you're in luck. If not, then make sure you are taking notes by hand instead of your computer, if at all possible. Writing out your notes by hand has been shown to improve later memory compared to taking notes on an electronic device (Mueller & Oppenheimer, 2014).

REFERENCES

Adragna, R. (2016, February). Be your own teacher: How to study with flashcards [Blog post]. *The Learning Scientists Blog.* Retrieved from www.learningscientists.org/blog/2016/2/20-1

Barbetta, P. M. & Skaruppa, C. L. (1995). Looking for ways to improve your behavior analysis lecture? Try guided notes. *The Behavior Analyst, 18,* 155–160.

De Vivo, L., Bellesi, M., Marshall, W., Bushong, E.A., Ellisman, M. H., Tunoni, G., & Cirelli, C. (2017). Ultrastructural evidence for synaptic scaling across the wake/sleep cycle. *Science, 355,* 507–510.

Konrad, M., Joseph, L. M., & Eveleigh, E. (2009). A meta-analytic review of guided notes. *Education and Treatment of Children, 32,* 421–444.

Mazza, S., Gerbier, E., Gustin, M., Kasikci, Z., Koenig, O., Toppino, T. C., & Magnin, M. (2016). Relearn faster and retain longer: Along with practice, sleep makes perfect. *Psychological Science, 27,* 1321–1330.

McLellan, T. M., Caldwell, J. A., & Lieberman, H. R. (2016). A review of caffeine's effects on cognitive, physical and occupational performance. *Neuroscience & Biobehavioral Reviews, 71,* 294–312.

Mueller, P. A., & Oppenheimer, D. M. (2014). The pen is mightier than the keyboard: Advantages of longhand over laptop note taking. *Psychological Science, 25,* 1159–1168.

Smith, M., Robinson, L., & Segal, R. (2016, June). How much sleep do you need? *HelpGuide.org.* Retrieved from www.helpguide.org/articles/sleep/how-much-sleep-do-you-need.htm

SPACING	ELABORATION	CONCRETE EX	VISUALS	RETRIEVAL
At the beginning of the school year or each semester, help your child plan out a study schedule, and help them stick to it throughout the year.	When your child is doing their homework, ask them how the things they are learning now relate to what they learned earlier in the school year.	Try to point out concrete examples in your environment that might relate to what your child is studying at school.	Help your child represent the concepts they are learning both visually and verbally, using simple sketches and explanations. You can take turns drawing and describing concepts with your child, making it into a game.	If you can encourage your child to describe and explain the information from their memory, then you are helping them practice retrieval and reinforce what they've learned.

TIPS FOR PARENTS

*We know many parents are interested in
how their children are learning in school,
and in helping their children learn at home.
We also know that many teachers may be
looking for tips that they can pass along
to the parents of their students. Here, we
provide concrete tips for ways that parents
can help facilitate effective learning at home.*

PLANNING (SPACING)

Your children will learn more if their practice
with the material they are encountering at
school is spaced out over time. Repetition is
important, but repetition is most effective when
the presentation of information is spaced out
over time. Therefore, it is important for students
to revisit older information in addition to going
over the most recently learned information.

Another way to think about this is that spacing
out studying is more efficient. When your
children cram, they may be wasting their time
doing something that is not going to help their
learning in the long run. We all know that time is
limited, and the amount children need to learn
is great. Short periods of practice at home can
help children learn a great deal. So, parents, here
are some simple ways you can encourage your
children to learn more by spacing their practice:

- **Help your child plan out a study schedule, and stick to it**
  At the beginning of the school year or each
  semester, help your child plan out a study
  schedule, and help them stick to it throughout the year. Explain to them why they need

to space their studying (you can use the earlier parts of this chapter for inspiration). What
your child should do during the scheduled
time will depend on what they are doing in
school, and their age. For example, younger
children can spend time reading or doing
activities from school, while older children
might self-direct review of material presented
during school to reinforce their learning. If
children get used to a routine of revisiting
schoolwork for at least a little bit each day at
home, it will likely be easier for them when
they have teacher-assigned homework or they
need to study for upcoming tests.

- **Encourage your child to revisit
  old topics**
  Repetition is important, but repetition is
  most effective when the presentation of
  information is spaced out over time. Therefore, it is important for your child to revisit
  older information in addition to going over
  the most recently learned information.
  When your child is doing their homework,
  ask them how the things they are learning
  now relate to what they learned earlier in
  the school year (or even previous years!)
  Doing this also encourages interleaving,
  which is also helpful to learning. Interleaving ideas (going back and forth between
  them) encourages students to see the simi-
  larities and differences between ideas. Want
  to go the extra mile? You might even ask
  your child's teacher for resources for your
  child or additional practice that your child
  can do to keep things fresh – especially over
  long vacations.
- **Take advantage of homework**
  Spaced practice is one of the reasons why
  homework can be so important to

encourage long-term learning in our kids. Ideally, homework should be giving your children an opportunity to practice what they have learned at school. As such, the goal should not necessarily be to "get everything right," but to make an effort to attempt the task at hand. Then, children should make sure to obtain feedback (either from you, or from their teacher) and try to understand where they went wrong. If you do give feedback on your child's homework attempts, try to make it about the content of the homework rather than how much of it they did correctly. That is: focus on how to turn mistakes into learning experiences rather than punishments.

DEVELOPING UNDERSTANDING

You can help develop your children's understanding about the world by bringing the following elements into your conversations and the activities you do together. These activities do not need to always be academic in nature – you can also help your child learn more effectively while playing or just spending time with them.

Elaboration

- Encourage your child to elaborate by asking them how what they learned in school applies to their everyday experiences.
- Find opportunities to ask "how" and "why" questions about the way things around you work. It's ok if you don't know the answer yourself – you can explore this with your child. But, do make sure to look up the correct answer so you can both learn it!
- If your child is working on a problem-solving task, such as in math or science, ask them to describe what they are doing on each step – quite literally, what is going through their minds as they try to solve the problem. This can help you see where they are going wrong, but more importantly, it will help them understand the process better.

Concrete examples

- Point out concrete examples in your environment that might relate to what your child is studying at school.
- For younger children, you should be able to obtain a weekly curriculum, where you can find the themes and topics your child is learning about at school; these could be a good basis for the concrete examples you point out.
- For older children, don't worry if you don't have access to their class materials – they're old enough to tell you what they are learning, which will help them because they'll be engaging in retrieval practice while telling you! See below for more about that.

Dual coding

- Help your child represent the concepts they are learning both visually and verbally, using simple sketches and explanations.
- With younger children, this might be something you are already doing naturally when you read to your child and they are looking at the pictures in the book while you read. Your child might spontaneously point things out in the pictures as the words you are reading describe them, or you can stop reading and make a deliberate effort to explain how the picture relates to the words.
- With older children, you can still take a look at pictures or visuals that represent the concepts they are learning at school. If you come across a picture that is relevant to what they are studying, save it and have a conversation about it with your child.
- Demonstrate to your children that artistic proficiency is not necessary for depicting ideas visually; show them how just a quick, rough sketch can illustrate a concept.
- For a bit of fun, you can take turns drawing and describing concepts with your child, making it into a game!

Reinforcement (retrieval practice)

- Practicing retrieval at home can be as simple as asking children at some point after school what they learned that day.

- It is ok if you don't know much about the material they are describing – just let them do most of the talking! If you can encourage your child to describe and explain the information from their memory, then you are helping them practice retrieval and reinforcement of what they've learned.

- You can also encourage *spaced* retrieval practice. When your child is doing their homework, ask them how what they are learning now relates to what they learned earlier in the school year (or, even previous years!), and encourage them to think back to the previous information in order to come up with the answer. By doing this, you are helping your child practice spaced retrieval, combining two of the most powerful learning strategies. Doing this also encourages interleaving – switching between different concepts – which can help students learn to distinguish between different ideas. For example, if a young child is practicing subtraction, it helps if they understand how that process is different to addition. Or, if a high schooler is studying differentiation, it's useful if they know how that is similar but different to integration.

- If you're having trouble encouraging your child to practice spaced retrieval through the homework they are already getting, you can encourage them to write out what they know on a blank sheet of paper, help them make flashcards, or help them make their own questions for retrieval practice. Just make sure that your child is actively bringing the information they have learned to memory. The activity may need to be adjusted if it is too easy or too difficult for

your child. In addition, you could even ask your child's teacher for resources that your child can use for additional retrieval practice.

Final tip: Make sure your child gets enough sleep! Even the best learning strategies become less effective when children are not getting enough sleep. Sleep is very important for consolidating, or reinforcing, what has been learned. Sleep will make your child's spaced practice more beneficial. Importantly, spacing practice out across the week (rather than cramming practice right before tests) can help alleviate the need for students to stay up very late studying before tests. So, spacing out practice helps your children get sleep, and sleeping more makes the spaced practice even more effective! Research shows that when students get a good night's sleep, they will remember more of the material they studied, and they will be able to relearn anything they forgot more quickly and more easily.

FREQUENTLY ASKED QUESTIONS

How much homework should my child be doing every night?
The rule of thumb, at least in the US, is that children should be doing roughly ten minutes of homework per night per grade (so a 3rd grade student in the US, aged 8–9, might spend 30 minutes per night on homework). This is backed up by research studies showing that it's not about spending more time on homework – it's about being consistent and doing homework frequently and regularly (Trautwein, Lüdtke, Schnyder, & Niggli, 2006). If your child is spending much more time than this recommended amount, you may want to speak to their teacher and ask about their reasons for assigning a heavy homework load – or whether your child might need some more support at school.

Is it a good or bad idea for me to reward my children if they do well at school?

Ideally, we would want our children to be inherently (intrinsically) interested in their homework and their studies. That's the ideal, of course – but it's not always possible. For tasks or subjects that your children are less interested in, small external rewards (extrinsic motivation) such as stickers won't hurt. However, be careful not to make those rewards too valuable, because disproportionately high rewards can actually decrease intrinsic motivation (Deci, Koestner, & Ryan, 1999).

What else can I do at home to encourage good study habits?

One of the best things you can do for your children is to model effective learning strategies in your own behavior. If you're learning something right now (be it a language, a musical instrument, or perhaps a presentation for work), make sure you are practicing it in front of your children. For example, Yana's husband was at one point studying for a Japanese test that was a few months in the future, and modeling spaced retrieval practice by using a kanji app that's based on spaced retrieval practice and interleaving principles. This way, he wasn't not forcing anyone to participate, but our children could see him practicing regularly and effectively.

REFERENCES

Deci, E. L., Koestner, R., & Ryan, R. M. (1999). A meta-analytic review of experiments examining the effects of extrinsic rewards on intrinsic motivation. *Psychological Bulletin, 125,* 627–688.

Trautwein, U., Lüdtke, O., Schnyder, I., & Niggli, A. (2006). Predicting homework effort: Support for a domain-specific, multilevel homework model. *Journal of Educational Psychology, 98,* 438–456. doi:10.1037/0022-0663.98.2.438.

GLOSSARY

Applied research (Chapter 1) – Research that takes what we know about basic processes and applies them to real-life questions and settings.

Attention (Chapter 6) – A limited-capacity cognitive resource that directs and maintains focus on a specific stimulus.

Attentional Control Theory (Chapter 6) – states that those who have better attentional control are able to more effectively select what to focus on, and maintain this focus for longer without getting distracted or starting to mind-wander.

Bottom-up processing (Chapter 5) – Information processing that begins and ends with the stimulus: you focus on the information coming from whatever you are trying to perceive, and you try to understand it just by piecing this information together.

Central executive (Chapter 6) – A component of *working memory* that is responsible for coordinating the other processes, but has not been precisely defined in the literature.

Chunking (Chapter 6) – Grouping smaller pieces of information into larger, more meaningful pieces of information so that they can be held in *working memory* more easily.

Cognitive load (Chapter 6) – The amount of information requiring our attention; the demands on *working memory* of processing information (see also *Perceptual load*).

Cognitive Load Theory (Chapter 6) – Sweller's theory of *attention* as it relates to education; the main tenet is that we can only process a limited amount of information at any one time, so we have to avoid overloading attention with unnecessary or extraneous material.

Cognitive psychology (Chapter 1) – The study of the mind, including processes such as *perception, attention,* and memory.

Concrete examples (Chapter 8) – Specific stories, pictures, analogies, and other items that illustrate abstract ideas.

Confirmation bias (Chapter 3) – The tendency for people to search out information that confirms their own beliefs, or interpret information in a way that confirms them.

Consolidation (Chapter 7) – The process by which new activation patterns that represent memories are reinforced after learning.

Correlational studies (Chapter 2) – Studies that show correlation; they can demonstrate that a relationship exists between two variables, but cannot prove that one variable causes a change in the other variable.

Curse of knowledge (Chapter 5) – Erroneously assuming that something is easy or obvious because you have had a lot of experience with it.

Declarative/explicit memory (Chapter 7) – Memories that we can access directly, voluntarily report the contents of, and are aware of remembering.

Deeper processing (Chapter 9) – Thinking about the meaning of information that is being encoded.

Dual coding (Chapter 9) – Combining words with visuals.

Elaboration (Chapter 8) – Adding details to memories and integrating new information with existing knowledge.

Elaborative interrogation (Chapter 9) – A specific method of *elaboration* where you ask yourself questions about how and why things work, and then produce the answers to those questions.

Empirical evidence (Chapter 2) – Knowledge that is gained through experimentation or observation; knowledge that is data driven.

Encoding (Chapter 7) – The process by which information moves from *short-term* to *long-term memory*.

Engram (Chapter 7) – A memory, represented in the brain by groups of neurons that are connected to each other by synapses and are activated simultaneously.

Experiment (Chapter 2) – An investigation into a research question where the researcher manipulates one or more of the variables (independent variable) and the resulting effect (dependent variable) is measured.

False memories (Chapter 7) – Memories of things that never happened, or happened differently to the way we remember them.

Implicit memory (Chapter 7) – Memory without conscious awareness.

Increased Saliency Theory (Chapter 6) – States that attentional resources constantly shift around so that some things become more noticeable or important (more salient) than others.

Individual interest (Chapter 6) – The extent to which someone is inherently interested in a certain topic.

Interference (Chapter 7) – When previously learned information interacts with new information in memory.

Interleaving (Chapter 8) – Switching between ideas or problem types while studying.

Learning Styles Theory (Chapter 9) – The idea that students learn best in different ways, for example visual and verbal styles, and that instruction should be matched to these styles.

Load Theory (Chapter 6) – Lavie's theory of *attention* that distinguishes between different types of load: *perceptual load* and *cognitive load*.

Long-term memory (Chapter 7) – Theoretically, an unlimited capacity process that retains information and skills over time.

It typically involves four stages: *encoding*, *consolidation*, storage, and retrieval.

Mind-wandering (Chapter 6) – Having thoughts that are unrelated or irrelevant to the task you are trying to pay attention to.

Neuromyths (Chapter 4) – A term often used to describe misunderstandings about the brain.

Neuroscience (Chapter 2) – The study of the structure and functions of the brain.

Perception (Chapter 5) – The subjective interpretation of sensory information.

Perceptual load (Chapter 6) – The amount of bottom-up information (sensory signals) that has to be processed.

Phonological loop (Chapter 6) – One of the three key processes of *working memory* that stores and also rehearses verbal/auditory information.

Procedural memory (Chapter 7) – Memory for tasks without conscious awareness.

Processing Speed Theory (Chapter 6) – Describes our attentional resources in terms of how quickly we can process information.

Prospective memory (Chapter 7) – Allows us to be able to plan to do something

Qualitative data (Chapter 2) – Data that are not inherently numeric (e.g., words, pictures).

Quantitative data (Chapter 2) – Data that are numeric or can be relatively easily transformed into numerical information.

Randomized controlled trial (Chapter 2) – Experimental manipulations that include a control group and a group where one variable is manipulated, random assignment of participants (or students) to each condition to create equivalent groups, and measurement of at least one dependent variable to see if the manipulation caused a change.

Refutational teaching (Chapter 4) – Includes three stages: facts, refutation, and inoculation.

Begins with presenting correct information, introduces the misinformation, and then explains why the misinformation is incorrect.

Retrieval cues (Chapter 7) – Hints that help you to recall a certain memory.

Retrieval practice (Chapter 8) – Bringing learned information to mind from *long-term memory*.

Scaffolded retrieval tasks (Chapter 10) – *Retrieval practice* tasks that are made easier with *retrieval cues* or hints.

Schema (Chapter 7) – Pre-determined categorizations of the world and the behavior of objects and people.

Self-explanation (Chapter 9) – A study strategy by which students try to explain out loud the steps that they are taking as they solve a problem.

Sensation (Chapter 5) – Objective signals received by your organs through the five senses (vision, hearing, touch, taste, and smell).

Shallow processing (Chapter 9) – Analyzing information with regard to surface or superficial details.

Short-term memory (Chapter 6) – A small temporary storage capacity with a moving 15–30-second window.

Situational interest (Chapter 6) – The extent which you find environmental factors engaging, such as how absorbing a text is or how enjoyable you are finding a lecture.

Source Monitoring Framework (Chapter 7) – A theoretical framework that explains how we attribute sources to our memories, sometimes attributing memories to incorrect sources, e.g.,

thinking something actually happened to you when it was just a dream.

Spaced practice (Chapter 8) – Having multiple opportunities to study or practice something at two distinct time-points.

Task-switching costs (Chapter 6) – Decreased efficiency and slowed reaction times that result from trying to go between two or more different tasks.

Testing effect (Chapter 10) – The benefit to learning from practicing retrieval.

Test-potentiated learning (Chapter 10) – The finding that later learning from reading is enhanced after a test.

Top-down processing (Chapter 5) – Using your knowledge to understand something, instead of just relying on the stimulus; bringing your prior knowledge to bear on your interpretation of the input you are receiving.

Visuospatial sketchpad (Chapter 6) – Helps you store visual information, plan using visual imagery, and create mental maps and spatial images.

Within-subjects design (Chapter 2) – Each individual participating in the *experiment* is serving as their own control; each subject participates in all of the conditions.

Working memory (Chapter 6) – A theory developed from *short-term memory* and made up of three key processes: the *phonological loop*, the *visuospatial sketchpad*, and the *central executive*. It allows us to hold information for a short time, manipulate it, and send it to/from *long-term memory*.

Working Memory Theory of attention (Chapter 6) – States that the amount of "attentional resources" we have is dependent on how much information we can hold and manipulate at any one time.

INDEX

Bold page numbers refer to images and tables

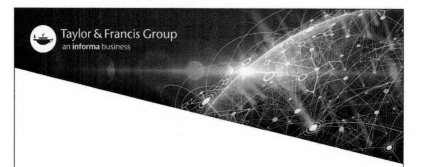